C000057006

Duncan of Camperdown

NEIL DUNCAN

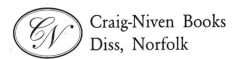

Craig-Niven Books
Diss, Norfolk

© Neil Duncan 1995

Published by Craig-Niven Books
March House, 12 Victoria Close
Diss, Norfolk, IP22 3JH

British Library Cataloguing in Publication Data
Duncan, Neil
Duncan of Camperdown
I. Title
359.331092

ISBN 0-9525650-0-5

Typesetting, design and book production by
Woodfield Publishing Services, Fontwell, Sussex, UK.

Printed and Bound in Great Britain

Front cover illustration:
Admiral Viscount Duncan of Camperdown, Baron of Lundie 1731–1804 (from a painting by
J.S. Copley, 1737–1815). *By kind permission of the National Maritime Museum, London.*

CONTENTS

AUTHOR'S NOTE

Whilst a great deal is known about the later life of Admiral Lord Duncan of Camperdown, there is little detailed information on his earlier years at sea. By researching conditions and customs in the navy in the eighteenth century, the duties and responsibilities Duncan would acquire as he progressed up the career ladder, the historical background to the wars in which he served and the detailed involvement of his ships in each relevant expedition, I have endeavoured to establish the pattern of his life over the fifty-four years he spent as a naval officer. Rather than being a biography, this book reconstructs the Life and Times of Admiral Lord Duncan using all available information, sometimes augmented by appropriate historically correct detail, to reflect specific incidents more graphically than would otherwise be possible were I restricted to a mere recital of the factual outline of events. I acknowledge with thanks the help received from the late Brigadier Henry Nevay Crawford MBE, Mrs Philippa Crawford, the City of Dundee Library and Museum Departments, The Forfar Library, Mr John Entwistle, Mr Eric Humby, Mrs Elspeth Johnson, Mrs Margaret Johnston, Mrs Patricia Kerr, Mr Christopher Gray of the National Maritime Museum, London, the Norfolk Library, the Rev. Martyn R.H. Thomas, Mr Ivan W. Warne and the numerous authors whose works were referred to and which are listed at the end of the text.

I am especially indebted to the late Brigadier Crawford for permission to reproduce the letter from Admiral Lord Nelson to Lord Duncan's younger surviving son, Lieutenant the Honourable Henry Duncan. Also to Mr Eric Miles for his artist's impression of Lundie Castle and to the National Maritime Museum, London for permission to reproduce the colour prints included in the book. My grateful thanks go to my wife for her work and advice on the manuscript.

Neil Duncan
Norfolk, 1995

PREFACE

The year 1997 not only marks the Two Hundredth Anniversary of the Battle of Camperdown, when Admiral Adam Duncan's victory lifted the threat of invasion from Great Britain, but it also marks the Two Hundredth Anniversary of the Naval Mutiny which spread to ships in Duncan's North Sea Fleet. Although never admitting it in front of the men themselves, Duncan supported the majority of their demands. In fact, two years earlier, always mindful of the wellbeing of the men of the lower deck, he had recommended to the Admiralty that changes be made which were similar to those later asked for by the mutineers. His advice was not taken.

With the threat of being foresaken by his men and ships on the one hand, and the threat of a continental enemy concentrating its naval and military forces for an invasion of Britain on the other, Duncan repaired on board every ship in his fleet, hoisted his flag and spoke openly and without fear to each crew. He respected his men and had their welfare at heart. They knew it and, in time, they responded to his call.

Whilst, at first, the majority hesitated [since they did not wish to appear lacking in support for their cause], leaving Duncan with his flagship and one other sail of the line to blockade the enemy in the Texel, they later followed him into battle at Camperdown where a daring, hard-fought and magnificent victory was won and where those who had mutinied redeemed themselves and received Duncan's forgiveness.

Admiral Duncan's handling of the mutiny was regarded by the Prime Minister of the day as his greatest achievement. Had he failed, the long-term consequences for the security of Great Britain would have been disastrous. Ahead of its time, it was a model for the correct management approach to a major industrial dispute

But his victory in the sea battle at Camperdown gave Duncan a place in history as a dashing, courageous, humane and courteous naval commander who was worthy of the brave sailors he knew it was his duty and privilege to command. As Admiral Nelson wrote at the time of Duncan's death: "The name of Duncan will never be forgot [sic] by Britain and in particular by its Navy".

Victory Octr. 4th 1804

My Dear Sir

There is no Man who more
sincerely laments the heavy loss you
have sustained than myself but the
name of Duncan will never be forgot
by Britain and in particular by its
Navy, in which Service the remembrance
of your Worthy Father will I am sure
grow up in You, I am sorry not to
have a good Sloop to give You, but still
an opening offers which I think will
ensure Your confirmation as a Commr.
It is occasioned by the very ill state

Honb: H. Duncan   of

health of Captn Corbett of the Bittern who has requested a few Weeks leave to reside on Shore at the Hospital, You will be confirmed before He resumes his Command

You had better get your things on board the Seahorse this afternoon as She will go to Malta in the Morning

I am Ever my Dear Sir with every kind Wish most faithfully Your

Nelson & Bronté

A letter from Vice-Admiral Lord Nelson of Bronté to Admiral Viscount Duncan's son on the occasion of Lord Duncan's death. Written in Nelson's own hand, on board his flagship HMS *Victory*, 4th October 1804.

Chapter 1 • THE EARLY YEARS

ADAM DUNCAN WAS BORN IN DUNDEE on the first day of July, 1731. His actions later in life were to inspire Admiral Lord Nelson to write: "the name Duncan will never be forgot [sic] by Britain and in particular by its Navy."

The Duncan family spent the summer months on the estate at Lundie and retired during the winter to their house at the end of Seagait in Dundee. At that time, the population of Dundee did not exceed six thousand and it was one of the best trading towns in Scotland. It had four good streets, a large market place and many buildings of wooden construction. Although they were regarded as landed gentry, the Duncan family lived frugally. Rents from the estate brought in little cash since a substantial proportion was paid by the tenants in kind. The furniture in Lundie Castle and in the house in Dundee was simple, carpets and curtains being found only in drawing and dining rooms. Most of the beds were of the box type, recessed into the walls. Generally, rooms had low ceilings and bare plaster walls.

The Duncans were strongly Presbyterian and, like others of that denomination, they endorsed thriftiness, sobriety, humility and respect for authority. When resident in the country they were regular attenders at the little church at Lundie where, in earlier times, communion had been served to the lepers in the community through a small window in the wall.

By the time Adam was nine years old, Britain was at war with France and Spain. The attempts of these two countries to dismember Austria found no favour with the British government which saw Austria as playing an important role in counteracting the aspirations of the French. There was great rivalry world-wide between Britain and France, both countries being intent on expanding their trade with North America, the West Indies and the East Indies. Sea power was vital to Britain's strategy and her navy could muster three hundred and thirty-six ships of the line compared with a combined total for France and Spain of only fifty-three.

The exploits of Commodore George Anson's squadron of ships on its four-year round the world voyage with the object of attacking Spain's distant settlements aroused the interest of many boys in the sea and ships. Although hundreds of Anson's sailors died from scurvy during the voyage, those who survived arrived back on the 15th April 1744 with the largest amount of booty ever to be carried in a British ship. Amongst the survivors was a son of the Earl of Albemarle, the Honourable Augustus Keppel, who was later to play such a vital role in Adam Duncan's life.

1744 also saw the French attempt an invasion of Britain, their fleet advancing up the English Channel to cover the crossing to the Thames estuary of an army led by the Marechal de Saxe. Storms created havoc amongst the French ships already at sea whilst other craft assembling for the invasion on the French coast were seriously damaged. Although this operation was aborted, disruptive efforts by the French continued, taking a different form and one which was later to involve Adam Duncan. With the connivance of the French government, wealthy Franco-Irish shipowners were, by this time, taking an interest in the ambition of Prince Charles Edward Stuart to regain the throne of Britain for his father. The enormously wealthy slave trader, Antoine Walsh, made his light frigate, *Le du Teillay*, available to the prince for a voyage to Scotland. The Franco-Irish shipowner, Walter Ruttledge, chartered the sixty-four gun ship *L'Elisabeth* from the French Ministry of Marine and, backed financially by Walsh, embarked weapons and sixty volunteer officers of the French Navy.

By the 2nd July 1745, *L'Elisabeth* and *Le du Teilley*, the latter conveying Prince Charles Edward Stuart and his retinue, were off Belle-Isle intending to pass to the West of Ireland and land the prince on the coast of Scotland. However, on 9th July, the British fifty-eight gun ship HMS *Lyon* intercepted the two French vessels in the Bay of Biscay. The action which followed was intense and both the *Lyon* and *L'Elisabeth* were disabled. The expedition had suffered a major blow with the loss of the arms and men aboard *L'Elisabeth* but *Le du Teilley* slipped away from the scene of the action to continue her voyage. On the 25th July 1745, Prince Charles landed on the shores of Loch nan Uamh between Arisaig and Moidart and the Jacobite rebellion had begun. His standard was raised at Glenfinnan on the 19th August and, on the 8th September, rebel troops entered Dundee.

Adam Duncan's father was provost of the burgh at that time and, unlike many of the gentry of the district, he was loyal to King George and strongly opposed to the Stuarts. Despite the presence of the rebels, he ordered King George's birthday on the 13th October to be celebrated by the lighting of bonfires and the drinking of the king's health. The loyal citizens of Dundee succeeded in driving the rebel governor, David Fotheringham, out of the burgh. However, he and his Jacobite supporters exerted a tighter control over the population on their return and discretion required the adoption of a lower profile by the Duncan family and others.

During the months of September and October, numerous French privateer sloops sailed from Dunkirk, successfully landing volunteer officers from the Irish Regiments of the French Army at Montrose and Stonehaven. Arms and Swedish field guns were included in their cargos, all sent in furtherance of Prince Charles Edward's cause. Later in October Colonel Lord John Drummond and his Regiment Royal Ecossais with more detachments from the Irish Regiments of the French Army and some siege artillery designed to assist in the capture of Edinburgh and Stirling castles, embarked at Dunkirk and set sail for Scotland in two frigates, a sloop and five transports.

Warned by agents on the continent of the impending departure of the French ships, Rear-Admiral Byng in the *Gloucester*, Captain Rodney in the *Ludlow Castle* with, in support, the *Milford*, the *Glasgow*, the *Fox* and the sloop HMS *Tryal* (later to become Adam Duncan's first ship) were ordered to intercept. A great storm blew up and, as a result, the *Fox* was driven ashore at Dunbar, the *Ludlow Castle* was almost overwhelmed and the *Tryal* was nearly wrecked on Holy Island. The French ships were split up but one, with eighty-two officers and men of the Regiment Royal Ecossais, was captured, although others did succeed in landing their valuable cargoes at Montrose.

Having successfully marched as far South as Derby, Prince Charles' army was in retreat by early 1746 and his supporters evacuated Dundee on the 14th January. Adam Duncan's father travelled to Montrose to convey the respects of the burgh's population to the Commander-in-Chief (the king's son Prince William Duke of Cumberland), provide him with intelligence about the rebel forces, and to arrange for the provisioning of his army. A few days later, government troops (including the 55th Regiment in which Adam Duncan's brother, Alexander, was an officer) suffered defeat at Stirling at the hands of Lord George Murray's Jacobite force but this did not stop the highlanders' northward retreat, one division retiring through the Grampians, the other taking the coast road to Inverness. By March, the Duke of Cumberland's army was in Aberdeen and the stage was set for the defeat of the Jacobites at Culloden on the 16th April 1746.

Just before his fifteenth birthday, Adam Duncan started his long and distinguished naval career in April 1746. He was a handsome youth, well above average in height for his age, with high forehead, fair hair and credited with being free from affectation and coarseness. At Leith, he joined the two hundred and seventy ton sloop, HMS *Tyral*, refitted after the buffeting she had received in the North Sea the previous October. She was commanded by Adam's cousin, Commander Robert Haldane, carried a crew of one hundred and ten men and was armed with twelve six pounders and twelve swivel guns firing half pound shot. She was a two-masted, single deck vessel with only the ballast-filled hold as a refuge from the wicked seas off the northern coasts of Scotland. To survive, the young captain's servant, as cadets were called in those days, had to learn fast on a diet of salty bread and biscuits. His introduction to navigation and seamanship could hardly have been tougher.

Following the defeat of his army at Culloden, Prince Charles Edward Stuart had fled from the mainland of Scotland and landed on Uist on the morning of the 27th April after a night of the most violent gales. Playing a part in the prince's escape was another fifteen year old boy, the son of Donald MacLeod, the prince's boatman. Hearing of the impending battle, Donald's son had absconded from Inverness Grammar School, armed himself with claymore, dirk and pistol and joined in the fighting at Culloden with others of his clan. The prince landed on the wild and dangerous coast of Benbecula, staying there for two days and two nights before moving to Scalpay. The British naval force in these northern waters had been charged with the task of assisting in the prince's capture and with preventing French vessels from carrying him and other rebel fugitives off to France. Misleading intelligence reports sent some of the navy's ships on a wild goose chase to the lonely island of St. Kilda many miles out into the Atlantic.

By the 10th May, Captain Fergusson in HMS *Furness* had located the prince's small craft as it lay off Finsbay in Harris. The prince managed to evade Fergusson by steering into shoal waters near Rodel Point and heading for Lochmaddy. There he found another frigate at anchor. Frantically, the prince's men took to the oars and, after a night at sea, reached Loch Uiskavagh where they spent three nights. Then followed a march to Glen Corodale, between Beinn Mhor and Hecla, where the party rested for three weeks. On the 5th June, they sailed North to Wiay, a little island off Benbecula, and then walked to Rossinish. But the trap seemed to be closing as militia men combed the hills and naval boats scoured the shore. Again, the prince made for Corodale but later headed South to Kyle Stuley near Loch Boisdale where he arrived on the 15th June.

He was here when Adam Duncan, in HMS *Tryal*, joined the naval task force engaged in this game of cat-and-mouse. At Loch Moidart, the *Tryal* took on board a company of Guise's Regiment under the command of Captain Caroline Scott, known for his enthusiasm and cruelty in hunting out followers of the prince in Appin and Lochaber. The sloop then called at the Isle of Barra on the 16th June. Here, Scott's men were joined by redcoats from HMS *Baltimore* and, together, they combed the island for rebels. Afterwards, the *Tryal* conveyed the troops to South Uist where, on the 21st June, they searched for arms and money at the house of Alexander Macdonald, the Laird of Boisdale.

At this time, the *Tyral* was anchored only a few miles from the prince's hiding place but informants, sympathetic to his cause, warned him of the presence of the ships and soldiers nearby. Immediately, his boat was sunk to prevent detection and he himself took to the hills with a guide and Captain Felix O'Neill, the son of a Brigadier of the Spanish Service. By the light of a full moon, they walked to Ormiclate, then to Hecla where they boarded a boat and sailed to Rossinish.

The French government was anxious to assist Prince Charles escape and *Le Hardi Mendiant* was sent to convey him to France. She failed to make contact with the prince and, her voyage being fruitless, she headed off towards Bergen. Another attempt was made by *Le Bien Trouve* which arrived off Cape Wrath on the 17th June, reached Loch Broom on the 21st and Lochewe four days later. After leaving South Uist, the Tryal patrolled the Minch and, together with HMS *Glasgow*, she sighted *Le Bien Trouve* and gave chase, succeeding in coming right across her bows as she skulked amongst the islands at the mouth of Loch Broom late on the 26th. Rather than risk being sunk by the *Tryal*, *Le Bien Trouve* surrendered. For the first time, and within a few months of entering the navy, Adam Duncan had experienced the thrill of a victory at sea. One can imagine his excitement as the *Tryal* took her prize in tow and made prisoners of her crew of thirty-one officers and seamen.

On the 29th June, Prince Charles crossed the water to Skye dressed as a lady's maid and eventually he was back on the mainland. In the weeks which followed, the *Tryal* was employed conveying troops from one location to another and in patrolling the waters between Uist and the mainland. The weeks passed with the prince still evading capture. Interest in him was waning and, on the 18th July, the Duke of Cumberland left Fort Augustus with the main body of his army, leaving the Earl of Albemarle in command. The earl was the father of Augustus Keppel, one of Commodore Anson's round the world heroes who was later to become a great friend of Adam Duncan. What military work remained to be done was left to Lord Loudon's Regiment and seventeen militia companies. Within a month, Lord Albemarle had moved his headquarters South to Edinburgh and, thereafter, only the militia and some regular companies policed the Highlands.

The ardour had gone out of the man-hunt for the prince. The larger naval vessels were withdrawn from the Minch, leaving only the *Tryal* and other sloops. On the 18th September, whilst the *Tryal* sailed out of Stornoway as escort to two merchantmen bound for Liverpool, Prince Charles Edward Stuart was boarding the French vessel *L'Heureux*. Under cover of a dawn mist on the 19th September 1746, he departed unhindered from Loch nan Uamh and set sail for France. With his going died the threat of rebellion.

However, Britain was still at war with France and, for more than a year, HMS *Tryal* remained on station off the coasts of Scotland and Ireland in order to counter the threat of invasion by the French. Despite the rigour of their duties in the unforgiving seas, there was time for the events of the recent past to be discussed and pondered over. Adam Duncan was aware of the viciousness with which government forces had treated the highlanders. He knew Raasay had been plundered and devastated by Captain Fergusson's men. Cottages had been destroyed and cattle slaughtered, the carcasses often left to rot. He reacted with horror when he heard of the raping of a blind girl on Raasay. His Christian upbringing and sensitive nature could not condone such an act.

But, for the boy and his cousin Robert Haldane, the commander of HMS *Tryal*, events at that time had an even more personal significance. Adam's mother was the daughter of John Haldane of Gleneagles and a Haldane relative of hers was the wife of Charles Stewart of Ardshiel (Tearlach Mor Aird Seile - Big Charles of Ardshiel). He had been the Colonel of the Appin Regiment which had joined Prince Charles' army and, after the battle at Culloden, had ninety-two of its men buried there in one trench. Following the failure of the uprising, Ardshiel had fled to France and never again returned to Scotland. However, despite a promise to his wife from the commander of government forces in the area that she would not be harmed, the infamous Captain Caroline Scott (whom Adam Duncan had met a few months previously whilst transporting detachments of Guise's Regiment to Barra and Uist) plundered and burned her home, Ardshiel House, on the 15th December 1746. Heavy with child, Lady Ardshiel fled through the snow on a winter's night and, two days later, gave birth to a daughter. She was allowed only a brief respite before being forced to flee again from menacing government forces. Whilst Adam Duncan did not know of this specific act of barbarism until a number of months later, he was anxious for Lady Ardshiel and for her safety during his time with the naval force searching for the prince.

After seventeen months service in northern waters, HMS *Tryal* called at Greenock in September 1747 before sailing on to Plymouth where she arrived in November. Adam Duncan then heard his cousin was to have command of the frigate HMS *Shoreham* and that he was to go with him again as a captain's servant.

And so, in January 1748, Captain Haldane was piped on board the *Shoreham* and read his commission from the quarterdeck before the assembled ship's company. The crew observed him quizzically since they knew he was to have the power of life and death over them in the months to come. There would be no appeal against any decision he might make or against any punishment which he might award.

The routine in the *Shoreham* was new to Adam who had been accustomed to living and working in a sloop in which there was neither the time nor the need for excessive formality. The *Shoreham*, carrying twenty-four guns and, with a complement of two hundred and fifty officers and men, was hardly the same. There was a difference in the nature and skills of some of "the people", as the crew were called, since, by 1748, the war with France had lasted for almost eight years. As a result, sailors for the navy's ships were in short supply and it had become necessary for gangs to press merchant seamen arriving back in port, and also landsmen, into naval service.

There was a raucous night before the *Shoreham* sailed from Plymouth when, as was the naval custom, wives of the crew were allowed to spend the hours of darkness on board with their men. The credentials of some of the "wives" were not enquired into too deeply by the officers. Next morning, Adam stood beside his cousin and observed the activities going on around him as the *Shoreham* prepared to sail. Voices rang out one after the other, "All ready in the maintop, sir!"

"Ready aft, sir!"

"Ready for'ard, sir!"

Then the first lieutenant called, "Let fall! Sheet home!" and a mild breeze filled the canvas as men on deck ran with the sheets. The noise of cordage moving and blocks jangling resounded through the ship. Men rushed to grapple with the ropes as the first lieutenant called out, "Belay the tops'l sheets! Man the tops'l halliards! Tend the braces! Hoist the tops'ls!" and so the action continued, with the anchor cable being paid down to the chain lockers and the *Shoreham's* guns roaring their salute to Plymouth's Port Admiral.

The task of the *Shoreham* was to patrol the English Channel and intercept ships trying to leave or enter French ports. Two days out from Plymouth she was off the South coast of Ireland when a French merchantman was sighted, chased, brought alongside and taken as prize. Then, one day in February, after pursuing and boarding a French privateer which had run into Belle-Isle for shelter, some prisoners were taken but the fire from the French coastal defence guns forced the *Shoreham's* boarding party to withdraw prematurely. There was more success next day when a North Carolina ship, earlier captured by a French privateer who had put a French crew on board, was retaken. Towards the end of February, the *Shoreham* gave chase to a French privateer of sixteen guns. There was a running sea battle before *La Valeur* was captured and taken as prize to Plymouth along with her crew of thirty-three. Then, for the next three months, the *Shoreham* joined Sir Edward Hawke's Squadron and patrolled with it off Belle-Isle in the rough waters of the Bay of Biscay.

Misfortune struck on the 22nd June as the *Shoreham* lay at anchor in gale force winds in Plymouth Sound. A hawser broke and she drifted on to rocks. She sustained substantial damage and the crew were paid off on the 13th September.

In October 1748, uniforms for officers were introduced into the Royal Navy for the first time. In the same month, Great Britain concluded an unsatisfactory peace with France by the Treaty of Aix la Chapelle. Now aged seventeen years, Adam Duncan was ready for his next challenge.

Chapter 2 • MIDSHIPMAN IN THE MED

IN 1749, A FIGURE CAME INTO ADAM DUNCAN'S LIFE who was to exert an enormous influence, providing him with opportunities for achievement and smoothing his path to promotion. Born in 1725, Commodore the Honourable Augustus Keppel was only six years older than Duncan. He had joined the navy from Westminster School as a boy of ten in 1735, served for two years off the coast of Guinea and for three years in the Mediterranean before embarking with Commodore Anson on his famous round the world voyage in 1740.

Keppel had the advantages of both a powerful patron, in the form of Admiral Lord Anson, and aristocratic connections, his father being the Earl of Albemarle. It was to the Earl that the Duke of Cumberland had handed over command of the army in the Highlands in July of 1746 following the defeat of Prince Charles Edward Stuart at Culloden. By the age of twenty-four, his younger son, Augustus, had already commanded the sloop HMS *Wolf*, the twenty gun frigate HMS *Greyhound*, the forty gun frigate HMS *Sapphire* and, as well as being captain of the *Centurion*, he had now been appointed Commodore of the Mediterranean Station. Despite his youth, he had served at sea for fourteen years and there was no doubt in the minds of those who knew him that he possessed considerable professional ability both as a seaman and as a naval commander.

He was a slim young man with dark hair half covering his ears, prominent curved eyebrows, widely-set sharp intelligent eyes, long straight nose and small pointed chin. It was to him that Adam Duncan reported in January 1749 after going on board the *Centurion* at Spithead. With a displacement of a thousand tons, the *Centurion* had a complement of four hundred and fifty officers and men, carried fifty guns on two decks and was classed as a fourth rate ship of the line, the largest yet in which Duncan had served. There is no doubt that Keppel took an immediate liking to Midshipman Duncan and, as time passed, the bond between them became stronger. The *Centurion* sailed from Spithead for the Mediterranean on the 25th April but she had to put in to Plymouth for repairs to her topmast. It was the 11th May before the shores of England disappeared from sight. Sharing Commodore Keppel's cabin on the voyage to Lisbon was the young painter, Joshua Reynolds.

As a midshipman, Duncan aimed during this tour of duty to become proficient in seamanship and to develop his qualities of leadership and command. Eventually, he was put in charge of youngsters in the midshipman's berth under the watchful eye of the gunner. He did duty as midshipman of the watch and, on many occasions, took charge of one of the ship's boats. He had to ensure he continued to improve with knots, splices, bends and hitches. He received instruction on the compass, on handling the helm and the lead and on the use of the musket and cutlass. He helped in loosing and furling the sails, training at first on the monkey topsail yard close to the deck. In time, he was able to reach the topmast in twelve minutes.

The background to the mission of Commodore Keppel and the *Centurion* was complex. For centuries, the Mediterannean had been the scene of struggles between the followers of Mahomet and those of Christ. By the end of the sixteenth century, the Turkish Ottoman Empire and followers of the Moslem faith had populated the Middle East and North Africa. No crews, passengers or cargoes of Christian vessels were safe from the attentions of the privateers who had operated out of Morocco, Algiers, Tunis and Tripoli. The privateers were known as Barbary Corsairs, a name derived from the Barbers who originally inhabited these coastal lands. The corsairs were licensed by their governments to ply their trade, the monies from the sale of passengers and crew forming an important part of the revenues of these countries. The freedom of the more prosperous passengers could be obtained by the payment of ransoms. Christian privateers also operated and they were based in Malta and were active against vessels of the Moslem states.

With the passage of time, European nations became increasingly keen to expand their trade with Mediterranean countries but, because of the activities of the corsairs, it was always wise for Christian ships to travel in convoy or to be armed. Eventually, Britain, France and Holland signed treaties with the governments licensing the corsairs and their ships were provided with passes which were designed to ensure freedom from attack. Unfortunately, the treaties were not always honoured. By the beginning of the eighteenth century, the number of corsairs operating had been reduced considerably. In 1737, it was reported that Algiers was operating nine galleots and eight sailing ships carrying up to eighteen guns each.

However, there appeared to have been an upsurge in the activities of the corsairs after 1740, the number of armed sailing vessels operating out of Algiers increasing to twelve and there had been some infringement of the treaties with the British Government.

While the corsair's vessels could not compete in battle with a heavily-armed sailing ship of the line, they were very fast and it was difficult to catch up with one in a chase. They achieved these high speeds by carrying as few guns and provisions as possible, by using large sails and by careening, scraping and waxing the bottoms of their ships about every eight weeks. On each vessel, the *rais* commanded the sailors and sailed the ship whilst the *agha* commanded the fighting men who formed the boarding parties. Whilst some of the corsairs' vessels had been built locally, others had been captured and later substantially altered. The corsairs were always keen to make a prisoner of a ship's carpenter since there was a dearth of men with this skill on the North African coast. Any passengers on ships boarded were scrutinised to determine the likely extent of their wealth and their value in terms of ransom money. Female captives were always treated in a civilised way.

The matter of immediate concern to Commodore Keppel was that the *Alcaide*, or Governor, of Tetuan was holding captive the British consul there and twenty-two other British subjects. This was the latest episode in a long-standing dispute between the British Government on the one hand and the *Alcaide* and his superior, the Emperor of Morocco, on the other about unpaid ransom money for British captives released some years previously. The *Alcaide* had indicated that, until the disputed ransom money had been paid, the consul and the other Britons would not be released.

Keppel knew the situation in Tetuan was extremely delicate. The population was in a state of unrest because it feared that if the *Alcaide* did not extract payment of the disputed money from the British, sending an appropriate proportion of it to the Emperor, the latter would despatch his army to Tetuan to punish them. As a consequence, and realising he would be in great personal danger if he went ashore, the commodore decided merely to show the flag in Tetuan in the hope the sight of one of His Majesty's ships of the line would suitably impress the *Alcaide* and make him alter his attitude.

The *Centurion* sailed from Cadiz directly to Tetuan, arriving there on the 13th June. As she passed through the Straits of Gibraltar,

Midshipman Duncan admired the rugged mountains of North Africa on the ship's starboard side and, to larboard, the nearly vertical sea cliffs and other slopes which fall gradually to the water's edge on Gibraltar. He learned that Tetuan Bay was treacherous when an easterly wind was blowing but safe to enter and drop anchor in when there was a light westerly.

As the *Centurion* dropped anchor off the bar at the entrance to the bay, she joined a forty gun Dutch man o' war, presumably there in order to negotiate a treaty for the safe passage of Dutch merchantmen. The *Centurion* showed the flag in Tetuan Bay for the next seven days until the arrival of a sloop from Gibraltar with instructions for the commodore from the government in London. His orders were to proceed to Gibraltar and assemble under his command a squadron comprising the *Assurance*, the *Rose*, the *Fly*, the *Guarland* and the *Tryal*, sailing thereafter to Algiers as a matter of urgency. A diplomatic crisis had been created following the capture by Algerian privateers of the English merchantman the *Prince Frederick*, carrying bullion and other cargo valued at one hundred thousand pounds, possibly equivalent to about £17,000,000 at 1995 values. The commodore was informed by his government that failure to obtain the agreement of the *Dey* of Algiers to the return of the stolen cargo would result in more aggressive measures being taken against the Algerines.

Having assembled at Gibraltar, Commodore Keppel's impressive squadron of six ships weighed anchor and set sail for Algiers. Land was first sighted when the *Centurion*, wearing the commodore's broad red pendant at the main top mast head, was about fifty miles from her destination. Passing the steep cliffs and rugged coastline West of Tipasa, the landscape changed gradually to include some sandy coves, changing yet again as the *Centurion* approached the enticing beaches of yellow sand to the West of Algiers.

By mid-afternoon on the 29th June, the squadron sailed into the open bay at Algiers and the *Centurion* dropped anchor within gunshot of the *Dey*'s Palace. The white buildings of the town were aligned in rows parallel to the coastline, the mountains behind forming an impressive backcloth. The cannons of the Algerian fort fired a twenty-one gun salute in honour of the English king's men of war and the commodore ordered this token of respect to be acknowledged. On twenty occasions, the *Centurion*'s guns belched smoke harmlessly from their muzzles, the guns being filled with powder only when used in salute. Unfortunately, due to an error, the twenty-first firing sent a shot skimming above the surface of the waters of the bay landward towards Algiers. It was only by luck that it failed to reach the shore!

An immediate apology was despatched to the *Dey* and, on the following morning, Commodore Keppel and the British Consul in Algiers requested an audience with him. They demanded the immediate return of the *Prince Frederick's* valuable cargo. The *Dey* was in angry, truculent mood and, through an interpreter he demanded to know why, referring to Augustus Keppel's youthfulness, the English King had insulted him by sending a boy to Algiers. The Commodore replied, "Had my master supposed that wisdom was measured by the length of the beard, he would have sent your Deyship a he-goat!" For a few moments, Keppel's life was in danger as the *Dey*'s bodyguards moved threateningly towards him. Through the interpreter, Keppel suggested that His Excellency might care to look out of the window and observe the six English men o'war at anchor in the bay which had the capability to destroy him and his city before nightfall.

The tension eased but, by the end of the audience, nothing had been achieved. Whilst the *Dey* claimed friendship with the English King, he insisted any vessels searched by the Algerines had carried no passes to prove they were English and, in any event, the cargo from the *Prince Frederick* had already been sold and the proceeds divided amongst the owners and crews of the vessels involved. It was obvious negotiations with the Algerines and, from the earlier port of call, with the Tetuans, were likely to be protracted.

Since Britain was not at war, all of the sailors were volunteers and they were allowed off ship whenever possible. This was not the case with pressed men during wartime to whom such a privilege could not be granted since they were likely to desert. Sightseeing by the officers, midshipmen and sailors was a popular pastime during the next few days. In the city square, surrounded on all sides by turreted buildings, they saw groups of local people viewing the latest batch of slaves to be put up for auction. Most of these were of Greek or Albanian origin. Almost naked, the wretched fellows were handled and prodded by potential purchasers intent upon determining their strength, state of health and likely usefulness for work. Others had their mouths held open and their teeth inspected.

Midshipman Duncan's eighteenth birthday occurred during the *Centurion's* stay in Algiers. This did not pass unnoticed in the midshipmen's berth! As was common on important occasions, the senior master's mate made a *carouse*, the ingredients for which were curacao, sherry, rum and brandy, stirred, and with slices of lemon floated on top. The drink was accompanied by large helpings of pork, biscuits and cheese. On such occasions, it was common for the high spirits of the midshipmen to be expended in active games, a common one involving that, on the call, "All change", each of the youngsters at table would disappear under it, crawl to the stool of the person opposite and devour as much as possible of his meal before the next call for "All change". Each midshipman then fought his way back under the table to his original position and to what remained of his own meal. With as many as fourteen bodies in motion under the table at the one time, with the call "All change" being made several times during the meal and with enthusiasm increasing as the quantity of the *carouse* drunk increased, there was much rough play.

Following his audience with the *Dey*, Commodore Keppel sent a report back to London and, whilst awaiting further instructions, proceeded eventually to Port Mahon in Minorca. There being no satisfactory chart of the waters around the island, members of the *Centurion's* crew were kept busy accurately surveying many of its bays and anchorages. Unfortunately, the commodore was frequently unwell, a consequence of his long round the world voyage with Lord Anson some years earlier. Whilst in Port Mahon, a man called John Dyer was enrolled as a member of the crew. Towards the end of 1749, the commodore decided the *Centurion* should visit Gibraltar to check on the progress of negotiations with the Tetuans and she arrived there on the 23rd December. Whilst the Tetuans appeared to be adopting a more co-operative approach, reports reaching Gibraltar indicated substantially increased Algerine activities against Dutch, Danish and Swedish ships. Keppel's audience with the *Dey* appeared to have had some effect since, by that date, there had been no interference with English merchantmen.

Further problems did arise with the Algerine privateers and, in January 1750, English merchantmen were being seized on the grounds that their passes were not in order. It was usual for a number of English sailors to be taken off and replaced by an equal number of Algerines as prize crew who had the task of taking the ship to Algiers. However, the English seamen left on the prize ship usually managed to recover control before Algiers was reached!

The *Centurion* was back in Algiers in July 1750. Commodore Keppel was now in constant pain and he transferred his quarters to a house in the city. He continued his contacts and negotiations with the *Dey* and, in respect of the seizures of the English merchantmen earlier in the year, he obtained an apology and the assurance that the offending captains had been punished.

Midshipman Duncan found the cycle of visits to Port Mahon, Gibraltar, Tetuan, Algiers and later Tunis and Tripoli, involving sailing in sunny Mediterranean waters, a pleasant change from the conditions he had experienced in earlier years off the western coast of Scotland and in the Bay of Biscay. Inevitably, he heard of the desertion, whilst the *Centurion* was in Algiers, of John Dyer, the crew member taken on board at Port Mahon the previous year. It now became known that, in Algiers about five years previously, Dyer had deserted from a British ship and converted to the Moslem faith. He had married and had a wife and children in Algiers. He deserted them after a number of years to go to Port Mahon. When Commodore Keppel made enquiries following Dyer's desertion, he was informed by the Algerines that they held him but, being of the Moslem faith, he could not be released to the British authorities. The commodore was also informed that for deserting his Moslem family, Dyer would be punished by the removal of his head if the commodore agreed. Keppel did agree and the man was duly executed. Had he been returned to the *Centurion*, he would likely have been hanged or flogged round the fleet.

It was early in 1752 before Commodore Keppel reached agreement with the rulers of the various states. The British captives in Tetuan had been released and, at least for the time being, the problems with the Algerines had been resolved. On the occasion of the signing of the treaty with the *Dey* of Algiers, teams of sailors manhandled the containers of gifts including clocks, rings, snuff boxes, cloth and sugar loaves presented to the *Dey* and his numerous minions. That was the way diplomacy worked.

By the time the *Centurion* departed from the Mediterranean, all serving in her had become very familiar with the North African coast. She had negotiated the dangerous waters between Cape Bougaroun and Annaba, her crew had spent happy hours swimming from the fine beaches around Tunis, admired the olive groves at Sfax, the palm trees on Kerkennah Islands, the camels ambling over the flatlands southwards to Gabes and the flamingoes on Gerba Island. Sightseeing, fishing and bathing had been principal pastimes of the midshipmen and youngsters.

In July of 1752, the *Centurion* sailed into Lisbon and Commodore Keppel handed over command of the Mediterranean station to Commodore the Honourable George Edgcumbe. Whilst there, he received several visits from Captain the Honourable Augustus Hervey, brother of the Earl of Bristol, including one visit which lasted until the *Centurion* was almost over the bar on the 7th August at the start of her homeward journey. There appears to have been some dispute between the two officers over Keppel's claim as Station Commander in the Mediterranean to a third of the value of commissions paid by merchants to Hervey for the carriage of their merchandise on his naval ship.

Whilst captains, officers and crew could earn prize money from the capture of enemy shipping during wartime, in peacetime merchants paid a commission of about one per cent of the value of a cargo carried for them by naval ships. Only captains were eligible for such payments but one third of such commission had to be handed over to the admiral or station commander. With many ships in a squadron, an admiral's share could be substantial. In the argument between Keppel and Hervey, Keppel was claiming his third of Hervey's commission. To an ambitious, thrifty young Scotsman like Midshipman Duncan, the advantages of attaining captain's rank or higher at as early a date as possible did not pass unnoticed.

It was during this tour of duty in the Mediterranean that Duncan was given the opportunity to take control of the ship for the first time. It was an experience he always remembered. He had picked up the speaking trumpet and ordered, "Prepare to weigh anchor! Man the capstan! Hands aloft! Stand by to loose mains'ls. Stand by to loose tops'ls!" There had been a flurry of activity as men scurried to take up their positions on the forecastle and by the bars slotted into the drum head of the capstan. The shrouds had become alive with clambering men and, within twelve minutes, they had been in their positions on the main sail and top sail yards. Meantime, amidships and on the poop the waisters and afterguard had been preparing to haul on the braces.

Under Duncan's control had been twenty thousand square feet of canvas weighing more than six tons, twenty five miles of rope in the rigging and more than four hundred men. He had raised his speaking trumpet to his mouth again, calling out, "Weigh anchor!"

The air had become filled with the noise of cable briskly passing through the hawse holes, the clatter of blocks and the drumming of men's feet on the deck as they pushed on the bars in the capstan. Cable had passed into the lockers below to be stored and ready to be run out when next the ship anchored. He had ordered, "Larboard braces forward! Starboard braces aft!" and this had brought the yards around to the angle necessary to attack the wind.

"All ready in the maintop, sir," had come the call from the midshipman there, followed immediately by those from the lieutenants in charge of the fore and mizzen masts, "All ready for'ard, sir!"

"All ready aft, sir!"

Immediately the call "Anchors aweigh!" was heard from the forecastle, Duncan had ordered, "Loose mains'ls!" and shortly afterwards the air had been filled with the flapping of canvas. To the quartermaster, he had called out, "Helm hard a-larboard!" The response had come back, "Helm hard a-larboard, sir!" "Steer sou'sou'east!" and then "Loose tops'ls" which had brought a burst of activity from the men on the top sail yards. The tide had acted on the rudder, the sails had filled and HMS *Centurion* was under way, gradually clearing the ships nearby. Midshipman Duncan had known then that he could control a sail of the line.

But Duncan also kept watch by day and by night, supervised many operations involved in the routine running of the ship including the stowing of hammocks, making the rounds after lights out and heaving the log to check the ship's speed. He assisted the lieutenants in charge of each mast and took his place on the tops, commanded the ship's boats and supervised the practice firing of her guns.

The Centurion returned to England in the latter part of July, Commodore Keppel struck his pendant and the ship was paid off.

Adam Duncan returned to Dundee and to his beloved Lundie. The countryside around was essentially treeless and it had been only in recent years that some owners had constructed decent roads across their land. Agricultural methods were primitive and yield from the land was often inadequate to feed the local populace if the weather had been bad. At that time, the potato had recently been introduced into Scotland and another innovation had been the turning over of large areas of land to sheep. During spring and summer, the tenants and cottagers on the Lundie estate worked from early morning until mid-evening with one hour breaks for breakfast and at mid-day. If life for Midshipman Duncan had been hard at sea, so had it also been for those working the land in Scotland.

The midshipman's leave at Lundie included fishing for pike, perch and eels in the lochs near Lundie and, frequently, climbing the small hill at Pitlail renowned for its remarkable echo. Compared to the excitement of naval life, time dragged after the first year of enforced inactivity.

An artist's impression of Lundie Castle.

Chapter 3 • PRELUDE TO WAR

AFTER BEING UNEMPLOYED AND ON HALF PAY for more than two years following his return from the Mediterranean, Adam Duncan was made an acting lieutenant on HMS *Norwich* in December 1754. Promotion to lieutenant was confirmed by the Admiralty on the 10th January 1755 and he joined the *Centurion* with Commodore Keppel again in command. The commodore had just been appointed Commander of the North American Station.

Duncan now dined in the lieutenants' mess, had a berth of his own and a cot instead of a hammock in which to sleep. As in earlier years, Mister Owen was the *Centurion*'s first lieutenant and, from Mediterranean days, Duncan's friend Spendelow had also received his lieutenancy whilst the youngster Talbot was now a midshipman.

It was mid-February before the *Centurion* and her accompanying ship, the *Norwich*, anchored in Chesapeake Bay off the coast of Virginia. During the voyage, she had been battered by rain, sleet, snow and high seas. Day after day, waves had crashed into and rushed over her bows as she lurched repeatedly into deep troughs, water pouring through the bow-ports and hawse-holes. The sails were always wet and stiff whilst the rigging and ropes had usually been encased in sleet and snow making them difficult to handle. The sailors had been exposed to the intense cold of winter in the Atlantic and the violence of the storms meant they were soaked and blinded every time they went on deck. For weeks, they were never out of wet clothes. With the gun ports always closed, there had been neither fresh air nor light on the lower deck. Only the courage, alertness and skill of the helmsmen had made steering of the close-hauled ship possible.

The dark, wet, airless and insanitary conditions of the lower deck had resulted in many of the men becoming ill and some had died during the voyage. Like the other lieutenants, Duncan repeatedly advised "the people" to remove and wring out their clothing after coming off watch although the damp atmosphere pervading the ship made it impossible for it ever to dry out. Earlier years had made Duncan competent in seamanship, navigation and gunnery. On this present terrible voyage as a lieutenant, his concern was for his men and for their health and wellbeing. He was becoming known as a strict disciplinarian but he was also developing a sympathy for, and understanding of, the men of the lower deck.

Lieutenant Duncan was now twenty three years of age, six feet four inches tall and built in proportion. He had little time for small-talk, his conversation and thoughts revolving around the ship, sailing conditions, the people, places he had visited, his home and his family. He knew his father's estate would eventually pass to his oldest brother, Alexander, so he himself would have to be independent. He disliked waste and he hoarded any article including old clothes which he felt might be put to some use at a future date. His only reading was the Bible. When not in his berth, he spent as much time as possible on the upper decks since elsewhere on the ship he was forced to walk with head bowed and shoulders stooped because of the limited height between deck and deckhead.

The reason for the *Centurion*'s crossing of the Atlantic Ocean was the British government's concern that the trouble spot in the near future was likely to be America. By the end of the last war in 1748, the French had settled on the banks of the Saint Lawrence River whilst the British settlements lay along the Atlantic seaboard. Since then, the French had established themselves at the mouth of the Mississippi and in a chain of posts between there and the Saint Lawrence. They claimed the right to all the land in the interior of America, thereby encircling British settlements along the seaboard and preventing them from expanding inland. This was not a situation which the British government was prepared to tolerate so war between the two countries again loomed.

Great Britain's strength lay in her navy rather than in her army so the government preferred to avoid a land war in Europe. King George was ruler of Hanover as well as being king of Great Britain so, if the French joined forces with the Austrians, they would be likely to attack Hanover. If Britain lost Hanover and won the fight in America then, when it came to making peace, she would likely have to give up what had been won in America in order to recover Hanover! There was a risk that France might ally herself with Prussia and that Prussia would then invade Hanover, leaving Britain in the same position. Secret negotiations were taking place between Britain and Russia in an endeavour to ensure that if Prussia attacked Hanover, Russia would attack Prussia! Of course, the possibility could not be discounted that France would join with Spain and, in the end, Great Britain would be at war with Spain as well.

Labels on map:

NEWFOUNDLAND
St Johns
C. BRETON Is. (Fr.)
Louisbourg
GREAT
Quebec
ACADIA (Fr.)
FRENCH
St Lawrence
FRENCH
Montreal
Halifax
MAINE
NOVA SCOTIA
LAKES
L. ONTARIO
Fort Ticonderoga
NEW YORK
NEW HAMPSHIRE
Fort Niagara
L. ERIE
MASS.
Boston
CONN.
Newport
RHODE ISLAND
Fort Duquesne (now Pittsburg)
PENN-SYLVANIA
New York
Philadelphia
NEW JERSEY
R. Ohio
VIRGINIA
DELAWARE
MARYLAND
R. Mississippi
N. CAROLINA
S. CAROLINA
FRENCH LOUISIANA
GEORGIA
New Orleans
FLORIDA (Sp.)
GULF
OF
MEXICO
Havana
CUBA (Sp.)
JAMAICA (Br.)

Following behind the *Centurion* and the *Norwich* were transports conveying two battalions of troops under the command of General Braddock with the frigate HMS *Seahorse* in attendance. The intention was for General Braddock's force to attack Fort Duquesne and destroy the chain of French military posts linking the Mississippi with the Saint Lawrence.

Lieutenant Duncan's orderly and methodical mind was alarmed at the sight he beheld when the troop transports arrived. Scarcely one soldier was fit after the voyage. Each unit's arms and accoutrements had been loaded into several different transports so that every vessel had to be unloaded before any unit was able to assemble its own equipment. Like the other lieutenants from the *Centurion*, the *Norwich* and the *Seahorse*, Duncan supervised the unloading of the transports. The soldiers could give little help since most were suffering severely from the effects of the Atlantic crossing. The sailors had not fully recovered either, although it had been a month since they dropped anchor in Chesapeake Bay. They showed the strain as they struggled with the heavy tackles on the yards used to lift and unload the army's equipment.

The plan for the operation began to unfold. General Braddock with the two battalions he had brought from England were to be joined by three independent companies and six hundred local provisionals. They were to proceed up the Potomac River, cross the Alleghany Mountains and attack Fort Duquesne and the other French forts near Lake Erie. Because of the shortage of artillery pieces, four cannon from the *Centurion* were to be given to the army and these would need to be hauled over the mountains. Duncan's colleagues, Lieutenant Spendelow, Midshipman Talbot and thirty sailors were ordered to accompany the naval cannon since they were more familiar with them than were the soldiers.

Commodore Keppel indicated his intention to make his base in Williamsburg so he could keep in touch with General Braddock and, at the same time, help with the design of two schooners which the settlers wanted to build for patrol duty on Lake Ontario. The *Centurion* and the *Norwich* were ordered to patrol off the Virginian coast to prevent reinforcements and supplies reaching the French.

In July 1755, news spread through the *Centurion*'s messes that the French were fitting out a major expedition at Brest designed to reinforce their military power in America. In response, the British government had despatched Admiral Boscawen and additional ships to the American station. The Admiral was to replace Commodore Keppel since the size of the fleet would require a commander-in-chief of higher rank.

As Commodore Keppel lowered his pendant on the *Centurion* to transfer it to the *Seahorse* for his return to England, he received the news that General Braddock's force had been taken by surprise and routed some distance short of Fort Duquesne. Lieutenant Spendelow and Midshipman Talbot were amongst those killed. Four days after the battle, the general himself died of the wounds he had received.

It was the end of 1755 before the *Centurion* returned to England to find the country rife with rumour and those in authority in a state of panic. The French were reported to be massing large bodies of troops in Normandy and Brittany preparatory to invading Britain in a fleet of flat-bottomed boats. Austria, having failed to obtain the promise from Great Britain that British troops would help protect the Austrian Netherlands from the French, had allied herself to France. The only good news was that the United Provinces and Spain appeared likely to remain neutral.

France declared war on Britain on the 7th May 1756 and, shortly afterwards, Lieutenant Duncan was ordered to join Commodore Keppel in the *Torbay* as her second lieutenant. Whilst his tour of duty on the North American Station had been devoid of excitement, it had been hard and tinged with sadness. Obviously, he had proved himself worthy of the more senior appointment now conferred upon him and there was no doubt his commodore thought highly of him.

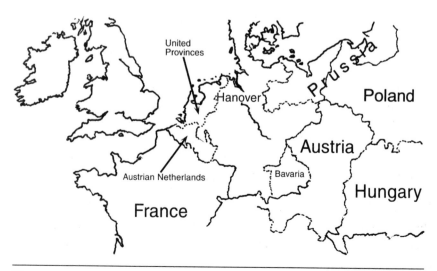

Chapter 4 • THE TORBAY'S SECOND LIEUTENANT

REPORTS REACHING THE BRITISH CABINET about the build up of French Army units on the coast between Dunkirk and Brest were creating alarm. It was believed the French were only waiting for the first dark night and a mild south westerly wind before invading Britain. Privateers were already swarming out of every French port ready to attack merchantmen sailing to and from Britain.

But there was alarm also about the intentions of the French in the Mediterranean. There was a division of sixteen thousand men ready to embark on transports at Toulouse for an invasion of British-held Minorca. To cover this eventuality, Vice-Admiral the Honourable John Byng, who had commanded the naval force in Scottish waters during the search for Prince Charles Edward Stuart, had departed for the Mediterranean in April 1756 with a squadron of ten ships of the line. These were all that could be spared because of the threats at home. On board were troop reinforcements for General Blakeney's garrison in Port Mahon. The general was now eighty-two years of age and largely confined to bed through illness, a fact which was not likely to be conducive to efficient operations if the island had to be defended. By the time Admiral Byng's squadron reached Gibraltar on the 2nd May 1756, the French army had invaded, and held strong positions on Minorca.

This was the situation as Lieutenant Duncan joined the *Torbay*, a seventy-four gun, third rate ship of the line, with a complement of six hundred and eighty officers and men. Not only was this the largest ship on which he had served but he was now, at the age of twenty-five, the second most senior executive officer on it after the commodore. One of Duncan's first assignments was to assist the first lieutenant to allocate stations to the crew. He also made a point of getting to know the various warrant officers on board including the master, who was responsible for navigating the ship, the gunner, the boatswain, the master at arms and the carpenter.

At the commencement of the war there was a shortage of sailors for the large number of ships having to be recommissioned. Press gangs were active, sweeping the streets and alleys of ports and coastal towns. Naval boats would hail, come alongside and board homecoming merchantmen, fishing vessels and colliers. Almost invariably this would result in some crew members hiding themselves in the hold or behind bags of cotton hoping to avoid the press. Often, they would be returning home after many months or years at sea, intending to spend some time with their families. Being coerced into service they would be resentful, disgruntled and prone to desert.

Although only seafaring men should have been pressed into service, a number of landsmen were always included, inadvertently or otherwise. Duncan and the other officers separated them from the seafarers. The 1756 press produced many small, weak, unhealthy fellows, some verminous and wearing filthy clothing which posed a danger for the spread of typhus. For these reasons, the landsmen tended to be unpopular with the seafarers who called them "Long Toggies" and made them the butt of cruel jokes. They were unpopular with many of the petty officers and, as a consequence, were regularly the victims of the "starting system" which involved them being beaten with a rope's-end by a boatswain's mate. Only when a landsman's own clothing wore out, and after he had been given seafaring clothes, was he accepted by the rest of the crew. The officers would classify such men, together with others who were unskilled, as "waisters", and they would live in the waist of the ship, look after the live pigs, sheep and hens kept on board to provide fresh food. They would also man the bilge pumps, handle the main and fore sheets and keep the waist of the ship clean.

Many of the men pressed at this time were virtually uneducated since there was no system of compulsory schooling. They possessed few natural feelings of tolerance and understanding for the men around them. These were times when animal baiting and torture were the main sports of many men in Britain who were oblivious to suffering, human or otherwise. When such vicious men erred, the infliction of harsh punishment was regarded as necessary since this was the only way they could be disciplined. However, the average sailor was usually found to be a good, generous, drunken, irresponsible fellow. If he got into trouble, drink was usually the cause. In fairness, it has to be admitted that even the pressed men fought well in battle. In 1756, the first of the boys from the newly-formed

Marine Society came into the navy. These were poor, starving lads taken from city streets by the Society and clothed before entering the service. It was a requirement that they should receive instruction in reading, writing and the scriptures. Later, the scheme was extended to adult men and, by the end of the war, ten thousand six hundred and twenty-five such men and boys had passed into the navy in this way.

The officers mustered the "idlers" who worked during daytime only, and these included the painters, coopers, barbers, butchers and the captain of the head responsible for the lavatory at the head of the ship. Men allocated to the "afterguard" worked the ropes which hauled the yards round to trim the sails and kept the after part of the ship clean. The "sheet anchor men" were the older and more experienced sailors who worked the anchor, the bowsprit and the fore yards. Only the youngest, fittest and most active sailors were mustered as "topmen" and they worked the sails above the lower yards, the fore mast section, the main mast section and the mizzen section. Men were also allocated to the Larboard and Starboard Watches.

From 1755, a ship's company was organised into divisions, each division being the responsibility of a lieutenant assisted by two or more midshipmen. The officers were required to make a daily check on the men's cleanliness and a twice-weekly check on their clothing and bedding. Divisional lieutenants also trained new men in the use of arms and in working with the sails and rigging. Generally, the new system resulted in cases of flogging becoming fewer in number and it created a better understanding between officers and men. Good admirals and captains endeavoured to ensure that ships were kept as clean as possible, that foul air was expelled from the bilges, that fresh food was provided as often as possible, that officers cared for their men and that they set a good example. Despite this, conditions on board were very unpleasant due to lack of space and fresh air. Whilst, in 1756, many officers still swore profusely, chewed tobacco and carried a rattan with which they could lash out at a sailor at any time, there had been a general improvement in their standard of education, manners and gentlemanly behaviour.

Lieutenant Duncan and the first lieutenant ensured the crew's messing arrangements were properly organised. Eight men were allocated to each table which was slung from the deckhead between two guns. Each mess had its own cook who collected its provisions from the purser and took them to the galley for cooking.

The *Torbay* joined seventeen other ships of the line in Admiral Sir Edward Hawke's Squadron off Brest as the summer of 1756 approached. Duncan knew from experience in the Atlantic that, even when the *Torbay* was sailing alone, the duties of the officer of the watch were quite onerous. Apart from being constantly alert for the vagaries of the weather, for currents and tidal streams, there was the log-line to run out periodically in order to ascertain how many knots the vessel was making. This was then entered in the log together with details of other of the day's events. However, duties were even more onerous when sailing as part of a large squadron, since maintaining station required continual trimming, making and shortening of sail. When sailing in two columns by night, open order required the columns to be ten cables (about one mile) apart, the distances between respective ships of each column being four cables. By day, close order was often used, when the distance between the columns was six cables and between ships, two cables. As each ship tended to have its own sailing peculiarities, experience and much practice were required on the part of the officers in charge of the watches to achieve exactly the amount of sail necessary to keep their respective ships in station. The sailors had to be continually on the move, now to get a pull of a brace or halliards, now to take in or set topgallant sails or royals as the special circumstances demanded. At all costs, what had to be avoided was a signal from Admiral Hawke's flagship ordering, "Keep station!" since this was always regarded as a reprimand for the officer of the watch.

When not required in peacetime, ships were laid up and it could take some time after re-commissioning before problems developed and were rectified. Similarly, it could take some time for a new crew to settle in. The *Torbay* experienced such problems soon after joining Admiral Hawke's Squadron. She had to return to Portsmouth for a refit and, again later, when an epidemic of sickness broke out amongst the crew. It was September 1756 before she was fully operational and, with the *Rochester* and the *Harwich* under command, proceeded to Cape Finisterre and thereafter scoured the waters off the coasts of France and Spain for enemy ships. The operation was successful, the *Torbay* capturing the *Diligent*, a French snow, on the 25th November after a chase lasting for many hours. Next, the *Anna Sophia*, a French store-ship with English prisoners on board, was intercepted. Two of the prisoners she was holding were the officers appointed to command the schooners which Commodore Keppel had helped to design during his stay in Williamsburg on Duncan's last tour of duty off the coast of Virginia. Immediately afterwards, the *Torbay* retook an English snow which had been captured some days previously by a French privateer.

Her next encounter was with the thirty-six gun French frigate, the *Chariot Royal*. There was a lively exchange of fire between the two men o' war from time to time during the hours of darkness, the *Torbay* employing her chase guns as she tried to shorten the distance between the two vessels. As daylight broke, the *Chariot Royal* again came within range of the *Torbay's* guns. The order was given, "Beat to quarters! Clear ship for action!"

With the scent of battle, and the possibility of prize money in their pockets, there was an urgency in the sailors' movements. Decks were sanded to prevent men from slipping. To reduce the risk of fire, water was poured over the hammock rolls, the sails, the boom and the ship's boats. Nettings were placed over the upper decks to catch rigging and men falling from above. Grapnels were made ready. Parties to board the *Chariot Royal* and ward off attackers were standing by with cutlasses, axes and pikes, waiting to receive their orders from Lieutenant Duncan or one of the other officers. Men climbed to the tops with muskets, ready to act as snipers.

"Brail the fores'l and mains'l up to the yards!" the commodore instructed, in order that these lower sails would not impair his vision and also to ensure they would not ignite when the guns were fired. Then, he added, "Open gunports! Run out the guns!"

The commodore decided to fire a broadside from his starboard guns on the up roll in an endeavour to damage the Frenchman's rigging since he wanted the ship as a prize. Were he to have fired on the down roll, he ran the risk of damaging the *Chariot Royal's* hull and sinking her.

Noise and smoke filled the gun deck as, one after the other, the guns roared. Flashes of flame were ejected from their muzzles after which they recoiled violently until stopped by the breeching rope. The *Torbay* trembled. Gun crews had neckerchiefs around their ears as protection against the near unbearable noise. If it became necessary for the larboard guns to fire as well, almost all of the crew of the starboard gun would move over to the larboard side. There were never enough crews for the guns on both sides of a ship to be fully manned at the one time.

During reloading, the starboard crews sweated profusely as they rammed bags of powder, wads and shot down the muzzles of the guns. Gun captains pierced powder bags and put loose powder into the flintlock pan. The men cursed as the guns were run out for a second time. Flintlocks were cocked. The firing lanyard was pulled. There was a deafening roar and the guns recoiled ever more violently the longer firing continued. Reamers were pushed down muzzles to clear away hot fragments followed by staves with wet sponges at the end to cool and clean the barrels. Then the guns were loaded again. The *Chariot* Royal returned fire, obviously directing it at the *Torbay's* rigging. However, realising she was outgunned, she struck her colours and surrendered.

Commodore Keppel and the *Torbay* arrived back in England with their prizes early in December 1756. The crew were in good spirits for they were entitled to prize money. Commodore Keppel would get three-eighths of the proceeds from the sale of the captured vessels, one-eighth would be divided between the lieutenants and the master, one-eighth between the warrant officers and another eighth between the petty officers. The six hundred and sixty sailors would share the remaining two eighths.

For the first few months of the year 1757, the *Torbay* remained at Portsmouth whilst Commodore Keppel attended the court-martial of Vice-Admiral the Hon. John Byng. Byng had been despatched with a squadron of ships of the line to ensure the safety of the island of Minorca. His ships had an unsatisfactory engagement in the Mediterranean with a French squadron on the 20th May, after which he had returned to Gibraltar, having decided he would have endangered its safety by leaving it unguarded if he did not do so. Also, there was general agreement amongst the naval and army officers present that Minorca could not be relieved by naval forces. Immediately news of these events reached London, Byng had been recalled and Vice-Admiral Sir Edward Hawke sent in his place. Byng was charged under the 12th Article of War which, in summary, is an indictment for cowardice, negligence or disaffection. If found guilty, the sentence was death.

John Byng was duly found guilty by the court-martial and, despite efforts by Commodore Keppel (who was a Member of Parliament as well as being a naval officer) and others, he was executed by firing squad on the quarterdeck of the *Monarch* on the 14th March 1757. Many naval officers were in sympathy with the inscription on his monument which read: "To the Perpetual Disgrace of Public Justice, the Hon. John Byng, Esq., Admiral of the Blue, fell a Martyr to Political Persecution, March

14th in the year MDCCLVII; when Bravery and Loyalty were insufficient Securities for the Life and Honour of a Naval Officer."

It was June of 1757 before the *Torbay* was in action again, first with Admiral Boscawen's Squadron and then on detached duty with the sixty gun ship, HMS *Medway*. The richly-laden merchantman, the *Commissaire General* was captured in July before the *Torbay* rejoined Admiral Boscawen's Squadron. On every occasion when boarding parties were required, Lieutenant Duncan was an enthusiastic participant, showing great qualities of courage and leadership. For the remainder of the summer of 1757, the *Torbay* underwent a complete refit in Portsmouth in preparation for a secret expedition in which she was to participate later in the year.

During August and the first three weeks of September, those on the *Torbay* saw the number of vessels at Spithead and in Southampton Water increase progressively until there were eighteen sails of the line, numerous frigates, bomb ships and forty four transports. Thousands of troops began to set up camp on the Isle of Wight. Arms, ammunition, equipment, stores, horses and field guns were loaded on to the transports and it was estimated there was one ton of equipment for each of the men taking part in the expedition. To ensure secrecy, no orders were to be issued until the whole force was at sea.

Admiral Sir Edward Hawke was the naval commander-in-chief. The *Torbay* was one of the ships of the Red Division, commanded by Admiral Knowles, to whom Commodore Keppel reported. The army commander-in-chief was General Ligonier with Generals Mordaunt and Conway as divisional commanders and Colonel James Wolfe as chief of staff. The army component of the force consisted of two battalions of relatively raw marines, ten regiments of foot each of seven hundred men, one troop of horse and two companies of field artillery.

The expedition left England at the end of the second week in September and, when the force was at sea, details of the operation were communicated to the participants. Prussia had now become embroiled in the war in Europe and she was engaged in fighting against Austria, one of Britain's enemies. The king's son, the Duke of Cumberland, was in command of the army in Hanover, endeavouring to ensure the safety of his father's lands there. He and the Prussians were under some pressure and the British cabinet therefore decided upon a limited invasion of French territory with, as its objectives, the creation of a diversion which would confuse the French high command and discredit the French government

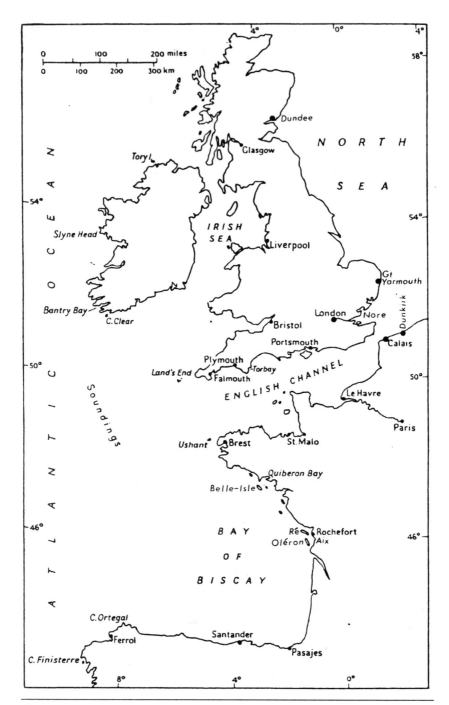

by gaining a foothold on its home territory. The site chosen for the operation was Rochefort and detailed tasks included the destruction of the naval docks, magazines, arsenals and any French ships lying there.

By the 19th September, the fleet was off the entrance to Basque Roads which lie between the Isle de Re and the Isle d'Oleron. The Roads narrow into the entry to the River Charente where lie Rochefort and the small Isle of Aix, the latter being part of the naval port, thought to be well fortified with coastal defence batteries. Admiral Hawke now instructed Sir Charles Knowles and his Red Division of the fleet, comprising the ninety gun ships of the line HMS *Magnanime* and HMS *Barfleur*, the eighty-four gun HMS *Neptune*, the seventy-four gun ships HMS *Torbay* and HMS *Royal William*, to prepare for an attack on the Isle of Aix the following day.

At four o'clock next morning, the movement towards the French coast began. At noon, Admiral Knowles' Red Division was ordered to take the lead and it came opposite the Isle d'Oleron around two o'clock in the afternoon, at this time being about five miles ahead of Admiral Hawke's Division. All ships of the Red Division were ordered to clear for action and the usual procedures were gone through. Some time after this, the *Torbay* observed a two deck French man o' war under full sail, unconcernedly heading towards the British ships, fairly obviously mistaking them for ships of her own fleet. Commodore Keppel hailed Admiral Knowles to warn him but failed to make contact. Lieutenant Duncan was then ordered to proceed to the flagship in one of the *Torbay's* boats to warn the admiral personally. He also requested permission for the *Torbay* to chase and engage the Frenchman, now identified as the seventy-four gun man o'war, the *Hardie*. Permission was given and Captain Howe in the *Magnanime* was also ordered to take part in the chase. Later, when Admiral Hawke's division caught up with the Red Division, he ordered more vessels to join in.

The excitement of the action took the *Torbay* into shallow waters until there was a danger she would run aground. It was clear the *Hardie* had managed to evade the British ships by running amongst rocks and shoals and into the River Garonne. Daylight was fading fast and no further action could be considered.

Early next morning, Knowles received a signal from Hawke to proceed with the attack on the Isle of Aix, although three of his ships which had taken part in the chase of the *Hardie* were still absent from his division.

In fact, the *Torbay* and the *Magnanime* did not rejoin Admiral Knowles until the afternoon of the 22nd September. Because of adverse wind and tidal conditions, no attack on the Isle of Aix took place that day.

On the morning of the 23rd September, with the *Magnanime* in the lead and the *Barfleur* and the *Torbay* following, the attack on the Isle of Aix commenced. These three ships advanced in silence, ignoring the intense fire they came under when the guns of the fort on the Isle of Aix opened up at noon. When they were forty yards from the island, the ships dropped anchor and, only then and for the next thirty-five minutes did they fire, pounding the fort with great intensity. As a result, the French flag was hauled down and the garrison indicated its willingness to surrender just before two o'clock.

British troops were put ashore to take possession of the island and to make prisoners of the five hundred Frenchmen who had manned the guns. The intensity of the gunfire from the British ships had so stunned the French gunners that many of them lay face down on the ground and could only be moved with difficulty. Prior to departing from their transports, all British army personnel had been warned against marauding and plundering when on French soil, failure to comply with this instruction being punishable by death. Within a matter of hours, those troops who landed on the Isle of Aix had broken into and damaged the local church, stolen the priest's possessions, devastated other properties and been guilty of rampaging through the island in a drunken condition.

The crew of the *Torbay* and of the other naval vessels now waited patiently for orders from the commanders of the force which would progress the operation. Meantime, it was known Colonel James Wolfe, the army chief of staff, and Rear-Admiral Broderick were carrying out reconnaissances, Wolfe reporting that Fort Fouras at the mouth of the River Charente was only lightly defended by a few French Colonial troops and Broderick concluding Chatelaillon Bay was ideal for a landing by the army. A Council of War was held on the 25th September and, although the naval commanders regarded the weather as being perfect for a landing, the army commanders did not agree to proceed. Three days of inactivity followed.

Eventually, the decision was made to land in Chatelaillon Bay on the night of the 28th September and thereafter to attack Fort Fouras and other forts in the vicinity of the River Charente. The troops would commence preparations for embarking on suitable transports and frigates at eight o'clock in the evening. At midnight the first wave of twelve hundred men would proceed to the landing area. As there were insufficient suitable vessels to permit all of the troops to be conveyed at one time, the boats which had landed the first wave would require to return for a second wave and the delay between the disembarkations of the two landings would be six hours.

By eleven o'clock, the first wave of troops had taken their places in the boats. The night was cold, a strong wind blew from the shore and the sea became rough. The soldiers waited in the boats, becoming colder and more impatient by the minute for a start to be ordered. After four hours, the message was passed from one man to the next that the operation had been cancelled. As the hour for the operation to commence approached, General Mordaunt informed Rear-Admiral Broderick, who had command of the vessels transporting the troops, that he wanted to be able to see the ground the troops were to land on. This would have meant delaying the first landings until daybreak. The second wave could not then play a meaningful part in the operation. A message was sent to the naval commander-in-chief, Admiral Hawke, informing him of General Mordaunt's decision.

On the 29th September, Admiral Hawke indicated he had lost patience with the army commanders and with the interminable delays. If there were to be no further military operations, it was his intention to order his naval squadrons back to England. A Council of War was held when General Mordaunt agreed to the operation being aborted. All who took part must have concluded it had been a disgraceful failure, largely because there had been no overall commander. Colonel James Wolfe, the army chief of staff and later the hero of Quebec, believed the navy should have proceeded directly to the Isle of Aix, that troop transports should have been anchored as close to the shore as possible and that the troops should have gone ashore and assaulted enemy positions without delay.

Commodore Keppel was ordered to leave Basque Roads in command of a squadron of seven ships of the line and cruise off the French coast. This he did on the 2nd October 1757 and between then and early in November when the *Torbay* arrived back in England, the squadron took several small ships as prizes, retook some English ships which had been captured by the French, including the *Levant*, and escorted a convoy of returning East Indiamen. In another search for enemy shipping later in November, the *Torbay* encountered a twenty-six gun privateer, the *Rostan*.

After a lively gun battle which resulted in both ships suffering damage to their riggings, the *Rostan* was taken and a prize crew put on board her. Of her crew of three hundred and twenty men, ninety concealed themselves in various parts of the ship, hoping later to surprise the British prize crew and recapture her. However, alert British sailors discovered and overpowered them.

As 1757 came to an end, the navigation of the navy's ships was made easier with the introduction of the sextant, an instrument developed from the quadrant, for measuring vertical and horizontal angles by double reflection through two mirrors.

News emanating from France early in 1858 indicated that a strong naval squadron was assembling at the Isle of Aix preparatory to sailing to America to reinforce French forces there. The *Torbay*, with Admiral Hawke's Squadron of seven sails of the line and four frigates, arrived in Basque Roads on the 4th April where they intercepted and chased a large convoy of French transports, most of which escaped. Arriving in the vicinity of the Isle of Aix, they found forty transports, protected by five French sails of the line and six frigates, lying at anchor. On observing the British squadron, the French slipped anchors and made for the safety of the shallow River Charente where most of them ran aground.

Hawke's Squadron waited overnight and, at daybreak next morning, found the French endeavouring to refloat their vessels by unloading guns, stores and troops. To aid the recovery of these at some later date, their locations were being marked with buoys. Admiral Hawke ordered boats to cut all the buoys free and parties were sent to destroy the guns and defence works on the Isle of Aix which had been repaired by the French following their destruction the previous September. This time, work on the island was carried out in a disciplined manner by naval personnel.

Admiral Hawke returned to England, leaving the *Torbay* and a few other ships to patrol in the Bay of Biscay under the command of Commodore Keppel. Over the next few weeks, the *Torbay* became involved in two actions. In the first, she chased the *Godichon*, a well-armed, fast French privateer protecting a convoy bound for Quebec. The *Torbay* came under constant fire from the *Godichon's* guns and from small arms fire from men with muskets stationed in her tops. Commodore Keppel was wounded but insisted on continuing to exercise command from a chair in the cockpit. Whilst he had hoped to take the *Godichon* as an undamaged prize, her resistance was so fierce that there was no choice but to order his upper deck guns to fire a broadside. The Frenchman suffered many casualties before she struck her colours and surrendered. The second action involved a four-day chase of the eighty-four gun ship, the *Formidable*, bound for Louisburg. A gradual increase in wind strength, a general deterioration in weather conditions and damage to the *Torbay's* masts permitted the *Formidable* to escape.

By mid-July 1758, the *Torbay* had joined Lord Anson's Fleet blockading Brest. Later, with the *Medway* and the *Coventry* under command, she saw and chased a large convoy of French ships which dispersed and took shelter in Port Louis, in Quimperley and in creeks along the coast. It was the 27th August before the *Torbay* returned to Spithead. Later, five of her crew were killed when fire broke out in her magazine, causing powder to explode.

In the preceding months and years, Lieutenant Duncan had gained much experience in a wide range of naval operations. He was acquiring a reputation for coolness and courage in command of boarding parties and in sea actions. He had confidence in himself but he never took, or allowed his men to take, unnecessary risks. Although he was a strict disciplinarian, he had the interest of his men at heart and they respected him for it.

Chapter 5 • NUMBER ONE

AS COMMODORE KEPPEL HOISTED HIS BROAD PENDANT on the *Torbay*, the crews of the ships in his squadron indicated their high regard for him by giving three hearty cheers. Because of weather conditions, it was the 11th November 1758 before the ships got under weigh. The squadron consisted of the *Torbay* with seventy-four guns, the *Nassau* and the *Fougueux* with sixty-four guns, the *Dunkirk* with sixty guns and the *Lichfield* with fifty guns, together with three frigates, a sloop, two bomb ships, two tenders and seven transports carrying seven hundred soldiers under the command of Lieutenant-Colonel Worge.

Keppel had been given the task of capturing the Isle of Goree, in the hope it would persuade the French to abandon their settlements on the Senegal River in West Africa. Being in overall command of the expedition, he handed responsibility for the day-to-day running of the *Torbay* to Lieutenant Owen, promoted to Captain as a result, whilst Adam Duncan was advanced to take Owen's place as first lieutenant. Duncan's duties now included overseeing the smooth running of the daily routine on board ship, dealing with disciplinary matters and ensuring the ship's papers were thrown overboard if ever the *Torbay* was about to be captured.

The daily routine was always the same. Coming on duty at four o'clock, the morning watch holystoned, washed and swabbed the decks. Breakfast of burgoo (coarse oatmeal and water) or Scotch coffee (burnt bread boiled in water sweetened with sugar) followed at eight o'clock. Afterwards, the forenoon watch scoured and washed the lower deck and this was sometimes followed by gun and small arms practice. The crew was piped to dinner of mutton, beef or pork and peas at midday and, half an hour later, grog consisting of a gill of rum and three gills of water was served. The afternoon watch carried out such work on the ship as was required before tea of biscuits, cheese and butter at four o'clock with half a pint of grog for each man. The first and second dog watches went on duty, one after the other, until the first watch came on at eight o'clock to be followed by the middle watch at midnight. The men sometimes entertained themselves during the dog watches by singing, dancing and fiddling whilst the youngsters and midshipmen rampaged or played marbles on the poop until just before "lights out" at eight o'clock.

In a ship with a complement of more than six hundred men, crowded together and with an official hammock space for each man of only fourteen inches (about thirty-six centimetres), feelings could run high at times. It was imperative for strict discipline to be consistently maintained. Slackness, for example by not ensuring that smoking was restricted to the galley, could endanger both the crew and the ship. If discipline was poor, bullying became prevalent and the youngest and weakest tended to lead miserable lives. On the other hand, if discipline was too strict, life for the entire crew became intolerable. However, there was general agreement that flogging, involving the use of the cat o' nine tails, was essential for the maintenance of discipline amongst the worst of the pressed men and for cases of insubordination. A captain should award no more than twelve lashes without the case being dealt with by a court-martial but this limit was not always adhered to. The use of flogging by the navy at this time has to be judged within the context that, in civilian life, even petty larceny could result in a severe whipping, and the whipping of youngsters in domestic service was also an everyday occurrence. A large percentage of punishments awarded were for offences caused through excessive drinking. For this reason, officers did not venture much amongst the people below decks, not because they were afraid, but because their presence might be the cause of a drunken man being insubordinate, with serious consequences for himself.

Therefore, the challenge for Duncan, as the first lieutenant, was to attain the correct balance. He was on the alert to ensure junior officers were not bringing men forward for punishment merely in order to create an impression that they themselves were very efficient. He was aware young midshipmen sometimes aggravated a sailor to whom they took a dislike with the deliberate intention of enticing the man to be insubordinate and, as a consequence, receive a flogging. To minimise problems on board, sailors had to be paid regularly, albeit pay had not increased over the previous hundred years. The provision of decent grog was also important and, whilst in port, women had to be allowed on board and discipline relaxed.

On the outward voyage, Lieutenant Duncan's task was made more difficult by the severe gales which increased in severity as the African coast was approached. The *Torbay's* maintop mast was struck by lightning and shattered, killing one of the crew. The sky alternated between being a blaze of light and being as black as night. The officer of the watch wakened Lieutenant Duncan in the middle of the night of 29th November when it was suddenly realised the *Torbay* was sailing very close to the Moroccan coast under these gale conditions. The crew was alerted and guns fired in an attempt to warn the other ships in the squadron of the dangers.

As day dawned and the storm showed no signs of abating, the awful events of the night became visible. The *Lichfield* was being dashed against the coastal rocks in seas too fierce for the *Torbay* to go to her crew's assistance. The *Lydia*, a bomb vessel, and one of the transports were lying against the rocks, both total losses. Men were trying to wade ashore, some being picked up by the waves and hurled against the rocks. A party of Moors arrived and were seen to strip the sailors of their clothing, afterwards making them carry stores ashore from the wrecked ships. (Those men who survived the cold and dampness remained in Morocco until a ransom of 170,000 dollars was paid by the British Government).

After a few days at Santa Cruz, in the Canaries, the squadron set sail on the 20th December, taking advantage of the fine weather to exercise in gunnery and battle tactics. The near-vertical black basalt cliffs of the Isle of Goree were sighted on the 28th December. The ships of the squadron anchored about four miles from the coast in eighteen fathoms of water. The foreshores were rocky which would make it difficult to get to the cliffs along the eastern, southern and western sides of the island. Where access to the hinterland was not protected by rocks, the French had sited coastal defence batteries, fortifications and entrenchments.

Having learned at Rochefort the lesson that troops should be landed on an enemy coast without delay and an assault commenced immediately, Commodore Keppel decided to attack the next morning. He anchored his transport vessels off the West side of the island. Flat-bottomed landing boats were hidden from observers on the island behind the transport ships and the troops embarked in these at seven o'clock on the morning of the 29th December in readiness to land on the island as soon as the Commodore gave the order.

Meanwhile, ships of the squadron had been taking up prearranged positions which permitted them to bring their guns to bear on the enemy forts. The *Prince Frederick* and the *Firedrake* bomb ship were to cover Fort St. Michael. The guns of the *Nassau* had the fortifications and St. Peter's battery as its targets. The *Dunkirk* covered a battery in the North of the island whilst the guns of the *Torbay*, the *Furnace* and the *Fougueux* targeted the batteries of St. Francis' Fort. Some of the ships experienced difficulties getting into position and they all came under heavy enemy fire. The *Prince Edward* commenced firing at nine o'clock but it was nearly noon before all of the squadron's guns were in action.

After that time, firing was intense. The guns of every ship in the squadron roared out, great clouds of fire and smoke being ejected from their muzzles. The noise rose to a crescendo and the ground shook as shot after shot hit its target. A dark cloud of smoke drifted across the island enveloping the fortifications. However, the battle was not one-sided. The enemy's batteries were active and the *Prince Edward*, a frigate, and the *Firedrake* suffered considerably.

Through a break in the clouds of smoke from the guns, the French were seen to have lowered their flag. At once, the commodore despatched his secretary and Lieutenant Duncan ashore to discuss arrangements for the surrender of the garrison. They returned shortly afterwards with the news the flag had been lowered in order that the two sides could confer and not because the governor wished to surrender. As Duncan was about to repair on board the *Torbay* from the boat which had carried him from the shore, a musket ball struck his leg and, after reporting to the commodore, he repaired to the midshipmen's berth where the surgeon cleaned and covered the wound.

Commodore Keppel immediately gave instructions for the bombardment to be resumed and intensified. After a short time, the French flag was again lowered and, on this occasion, the surrender was unconditional. Keppel gave the order for the troops, already in the flat-bottomed boats, to take possession of the island and marines were also landed from the *Torbay*. Prisoners were rounded up and put on three of the transport ships. The *Torbay* weighed anchor and sailed to Fort Louis where Lieutenant-Colonel Worge was installed as the British Governor of Senegal. Effectively, the French had been driven from this part of Africa, with the loss to them of the trade in gum, slaves, ivory and hides.

The *Torbay* arrived back in Portsmouth on the 1st March 1759. Not for the first time on his return from a tour of duty, Duncan found the country rife with rumours of impending invasions by the French, apparently to take place simultaneously in England, Scotland and Ireland.

As a result, he and the *Torbay* spent the summer blockading French ports to prevent such operations from materialising.

On the 21st September 1759, Duncan was promoted to the rank of Commander and left the *Torbay*.

For some months, Commander Duncan was captain of the *Royal Exchange*, a ship hired by the navy and used as armed escort to convoys of merchantmen. The new commander found his task exasperating since the crew, mainly of foreign seamen, considered themselves to be civilians and not subject to the discipline of the British Naval Service. It was with some relief that, following a request by Commodore Keppel to Lord Anson for his services, Commander Adam Duncan found himself promoted to Captain on the 25th February 1761 and ordered to take command of the *Valiant*.

Chapter 6 • A YOUTHFUL CAPTAIN FOR THE VALIANT

THE WHISTLE WAS LONG, DRAWN OUT AND MOURNFUL, the pitch rising slowly until it was high and piercing. Then, as gradually, it died away. This was the sound as Captain Adam Duncan, shortly before his thirtieth birthday, was piped on board the *Valiant*. She was a seventy-four gun sail of the line with a complement of six hundred and sixty five officers and men. Before the assembled ship's company, he unrolled and read his commission from the quarter deck. The crew were impressed by his large, athletic frame and his handsome features. He had come a long way since, as a boy of fifteen, he had joined the little sloop, HMS *Tryal*, at Leith in 1746, for now he had his first major command. His immediate superior was his friend and mentor, Commodore Augustus Keppel.

Soon after his arrival on board he inspected the ship's books and particularly the muster book to ensure it was up-to-date. He checked the quarter bills, allotting the hands to their stations. He inspected the ship itself including the arrangements for fire prevention and for the security of the magazine and the spirit-room. He examined the bedding and clothing stores and the decks for cleanliness and the adequacy of ventillation. He tested his men's capability on the guns and in the use of their small arms. He knew he would have to work hard for his captain's pay of thirteen shillings and six pence a day but there was the consolation of knowing his share of any prize-money would now be three-eighths of the value of the prize.

As captain, the ultimate responsibility for discipline on the ship was his. He reminded himself of the punishments awarded for the common offences namely, six to eight lashes with the cat o' nine tails for a first charge of drunkenness. Twelve lashes for subsequent charges of drunkenness, sleeping on watch, making a commotion and throwing food overboard. The punishment for refusing to obey an order could be up to thirty-six lashes but this would have to be awarded by courtmartial. From experience, he knew that, for a ship with a complement of about

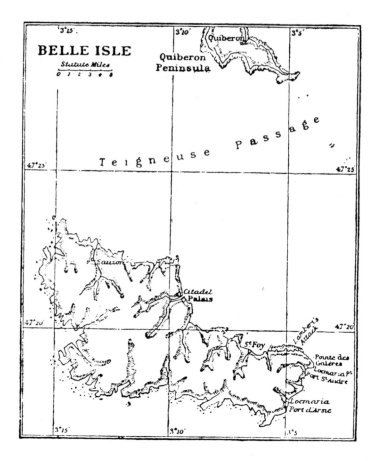

six hundred men, an offence attracting punishment by flogging might well occur almost once a week.

As flag captain, Duncan was in command of the ship on which Commodore Keppel was to fly his broad pendant. The commodore had a suite of cabins in the stern, on the deck below the one on which the captain's cabin was located. Keppel was now thirty-six years of age. He was greatly admired by Duncan, not only because he was a highly competent sailor and commander, but also because he was an agreeable man with a good sense of humour and strong views on Great Britain's place in the world. For his part, Keppel appreciated Duncan's relaxed and obliging ways, his coolness and courage in action and his enthusiasm for the job in hand and for the sea itself.

By March 1761, the war was going well for Britain. Operations in Canada had been crowned with success but in her fight against Austria, Prussia was close to the point of exhaustion. British efforts had succeeded in nearly destroying the French navy. An aim of the British government was to keep up the pressure on the French and, to this end, Commodore Keppel was to lead an expedition aimed at capturing Belle-Isle, the key to the whole of the western coast of France.

Keppel's force would consist of eleven sails of the line, eleven frigates, some fire-ships and bomb-ships together with one hundred transports. The Army Commander was to be Major-General Hodgson with ten regiments of foot, five independent companies and three companies of artillery. Keppel expressed concern at the employment on the expedition of some unseasoned regiments, in two of which he believed discipline and equipment were disgraceful and from which some officers were absent from duty. He wanted these regiments excluded from taking part in the operation.

The battle fleet set sail from Spithead on the 29th March 1761. Due to adverse wind conditions, it did not arrive off Belle-Isle until the 7th April. The commodore had sent four frigates ahead to intercept any French ships endeavouring to maintain communication between the island and the mainland. Moving steadily closer to the shore during the night, the fleet had rounded the South end of the island by daybreak. Being so close in-shore allowed detailed inspection of the French dispositions and fortifications on the island, leading both Keppel and Hodgson to conclude the ideal location for a landing was in the vicinity of Locmaria Bay on the south eastern coastline. However, at that particular time, the wind was on-shore and an assault there was not advisable.

Sailing northwards, the fleet passed Port St. Andre and Locmaria Point before changing course and travelling parallel to the North-East-facing shoreline where the principal town, Palais, was located. The commodore and the general explored further along the coast by cutter, looking for suitable landing places in the vicinity of the town of Sauzon which, after inspection, they decided was well-defended. Having completed their reconnaissance, they concluded there was no better location at which to land than Locmaria Bay after all, but wind conditions would require to be more favourable than they had been earlier in the day.

The plan drawn up involved the *Prince of Orange*, the *Dragon*, the *Achilles* and two other ships bombarding the French battery at the entry to Locmaria Bay prior to the main assault being launched there. For the operation, Commodore Keppel proposed temporarily shifting his pendant to the *Prince of Orange* and from her, he and General Hodgson would give the signal for disembarkation. To confuse the enemy, a diversionary assault by two marine battalions, supported by the *Swiftsure*, was proposed for the vicinity of Sauzon.

The battle commenced with two sails of the line bringing down concentrated fire on the forts at Port St. Andre whilst, as planned, others engaged the battery at Locmaria Bay. Officers and men from the *Valiant* and from other ships of the fleet organised the embarkation of the troops into the flatbottomed boats and navigated them to the appropriate landing area within the bay. Showing great courage, the soldiers did their best to advance inland. However, they, and others on the shore, were vulnerable to the enemy's fire from the high ground all around the bay. Its intensity prevented the soldiers from reaching and assaulting the entrenchments on the higher ground. Towards the end of the day, and after repeated attempts, there was little choice but to retire in order to prevent further casualties, of which the *Valiant*'s included one midshipman and eleven sailors killed, one lieutenant, one midshipman and twenty-six sailors wounded and one midshipman and fourteen sailors taken prisoner. Matters would have been worse had the retreat not been covered by fire from the guns of the sails of the line. It was now obvious the plan of attack had to be re-considered.

When the Prime Minister in London heard of the difficulties being encountered, he ordered out a further four regiments of foot, five more sails of the line, replacement flat-bottomed boats, stores and transports. Now the plan was for the main assault to be against Port d'Arsic where it was thought the cliff face was just capable of being scaled. This attack was to be led by General Hodgson's second-in-command, Major-General Crauford. The feint, which would be put into action first, was to take place at St. Foy under Brigadier Hamilton Lambert, supported by the guns of three sails of the line. A second feint by newly-arrived dragoons was planned for the vicinity of Sauzon, again supported by the guns of two men-of-war.

By the 22nd April the preparations were complete. The sails of the line were at their appointed stations and their guns were bombarding the enemy positions. There was a lively response from the French batteries and many of the ships suffered considerable damage. However, by three o'clock in the afternoon, the enemy's guns were almost silent and the army's assault went in. The first action, Brigadier Lambert's feint to the East of St. Foy, encountered no resistance and his troops advanced towards the high cliffs which the French obviously regarded as being impossible to climb. However, they were stealthily scaled by the grenadier company of the 19th Regiment of Foot and by a detachment of marines, all reaching the top without a shot being fired.

On the principle that success should be reinforced, Captain Stanhope in the *Swiftsure* embarked every available man in boats and despatched them to Brigadier Lambert's support. Shortly afterwards, units of Major-General Crauford's division were diverted around the coast to reinforce Lambert since their attack on Port d'Arsic, which was timed to take place slightly later, had not commenced. After recovering from their surprise, the enemy's forces put up stiff resistance but, by five o'clock, they were in retreat.

The French retired to Palais where they were subjected to a heavy pounding by British gun batteries established around the town. Several French redoubts were captured on the 13th May and, three days later, French troops withdrew to the citadel. After being subjected to further heavy and sustained bombardment, the French commander, Chevalier de St. Croix, surrendered on the 7th June.

This was a combined operation jointly led by naval and military commanders who worked together to achieve victory. The ships of the line had been used as mobile heavy artillery in support of the army. For Captain Duncan and his officers and men, it had been a test of their skills in gunnery and seamanship. It afforded Duncan valuable experience in the organisation of troop disembarkations under battle conditions which was to prove useful not very much later in his career.

The *Valiant*, as Commodore Keppel's flagship, remained in the vicinity of Belle-Isle with several other sails of the line in order to deter any attempt by the French to recapture the island. Ships' crews also assisted in unloading equipment and supplies needed by the occupying troops. Meanwhile, reports were received that the French were fitting out ships at Brest and Rochefort. As a result, Commodore Keppel organised blockades of both ports using sails of the line from what was now a very large fleet under his command. He also despatched a squadron to destroy fortifications on the Isle of Aix. For six months after the capture of Belle-Isle, the *Valiant* was the control centre from which all of these operations were directed and this gave the young Captain Duncan an insight into the command and management of large-scale naval operations.

It was January of 1762 before the *Valiant* was sailing for England. At four o'clock in the morning on the 11th of that month, she was hit by storms of gale force. Although using every available pump, water could not be prevented from entering the ship, as much as four feet accumulating in an hour. The pumps had to be manned constantly. This violent storm continued unabated into the 12th and, with five feet of water in the hold and the vessel on the point of sinking, she made the shelter of Torbay. Her state was so bad that the *Mars*, the *Burford* and the *Aquillon* had to be in close attendance during the last part of her journey. Other ships of the fleet put into different ports along the English coast, all in a devastated condition.

On his return to England, Captain Duncan found that Great Britain had declared war on Spain on the 2nd January 1762. Whilst France and Britain had been close to negotiating an end to the conflict during 1761, France had entered into a treaty with Spain which was not acceptable to the British government. In any event, for some time Spain had been acting in a manner unbecoming a neutral. The entry of Spain into the war was to have a significant effect upon the remainder of Duncan's career.

Plate 1. The attack on Belle-Isle, 1761 (from a painting by Dominic Serres, S^{nr.} 1722–1793).

By kind permission of the National Maritime Museum, London.

Plate 2. The capture of Havana, 14th August 1762 showing, on the left, Fort El Morro and the entrance channel leading to Havana Harbour (from a painting by Dominic Serres S^{nr}, 1722–1793).

By kind permission of the National Maritime Museum, London.

Plate 3. The Moonlight Battle off Cape St Vincent, 16th January 1780 (from a painting by Richard Paton, 1717–1791).
By kind permission of the National Maritime Museum, London.

Plate 4. The Battle of Camperdown, 11th October 1797 (from a painting by Thomas Whitcombe)

By kind permission of the National Maritime Museum, London.

Plate 5. The Battle of Camperdown, 11th October 1797 (from a painting by Philipe-Jacques de Loutherbourg, 1740–1812).

By kind permission of the National Maritime Museum, London.

Plate 6. The Battle of Camperdown, 11th October 1797 (from a painting by George Chambers).

By kind permission of the National Maritime Museum, London.

Plate 7. Admiral Duncan receiving the surrender of the Dutch Admiral de Winter after the Battle of Camperdown, 11th October 1797 (from a painting by Samuel Drummond, 1765–1844)

By kind permission of the National Maritime Museum, London.

Plate 8. Lord Duncan's headstone in the graveyard of Lundie Church (from a photograph by kind permission of Mr E.W. Miles).

Plate 9. The Naval General Service Medal 1793–1840 with the Camperdown clasp showing obverse and reverse of the medal.

Chapter 7 • THE EXPEDITION TO HAVANA

THE ENTRY OF SPAIN INTO THE WAR brought a decision from the British cabinet to thrust immediately at the heart of Spanish colonial power and wealth by means of an expedition to Havana, the queen of cities in the West Indies. Command of the naval force was given to Vice-Admiral Pocock, recently returned from India where he had played an important part in successful operations against the French and the Dutch. Commodore Augustus Keppel was appointed second-in-command with Adam Duncan, commanding the *Valiant*, as his flag captain.

The Duke of Cumberland had considerable influence with his nephew the king and, as a result, Commodore Keppel's eldest brother, Lieutenant-General The Earl of Albemarle, was appointed army commander. It was to the earl's late father that the Duke had handed over command of the army in Scotland shortly after the battle of Culloden. Albemarle was thirty-eight years old and had been on the duke's staff since the age of sixteen. Whilst he had never previously held a command, he was credited with the ability to select able men whose judgement could be trusted. Lieutenant-General George Eliott, an officer with a good war record, was to be his second-in-command. Major-General La Fausille and Major-General William Keppel (another brother of the earl and of the commodore) were to be the divisional commanders. Fresh from command of a brigade at Belle-Isle, Colonel Guy Carleton was appointed quartermaster-general.

The expeditionary force was to comprise naval and army units drawn from Britain, the West Indies and America. The plan was for these to converge and unite at Cape Saint Nicolas at the North West end of French-controlled St. Domingue. The combined force would consist of a fleet of thirty-four sails of the line and about the same number of frigates together with an army corps of nearly fourteen thousand men. The operation had to be completed speedily if casualties from tropical diseases were to be kept to a minimum. In any event, the latest date by which success had to be achieved was the end of August since, after that, the hurricanes would strike.

Preparations for the expedition had proceeded very rapidly since the 7th January 1762 when orders were issued by the Admiralty. Following the completion of essential repairs on her return from Belle-Isle, the *Valiant* was lying at anchor at Spithead by the 19th February 1762. More than four thousand troops and their equipment had also assembled by that date but they could not embark on the troop transports as no usable bedding was available and there was none in the naval stores in Portsmouth. That which had been returned from the Belle Isle expedition was either rotten, rat-eaten or worn out and replacements had to come with the ordnance and victualling transports currently loading in the Thames. These arrived at Spithead on the 25th February and, immediately thereafter, bedding could be taken on and the troops embarked. The victualling transports carried seven month's rations for sixteen thousand men.

The *Valiant* moved to St. Helen's on the 4th March and, at eight o'clock on the morning of the 5th, Admiral Pocock, flying his flag on the *Namur*, made the signal to weigh anchor. By noon, the *Valiant*, the *Belleisle*, the *Hampton Court* and the *Ripon* with sixty-four transports and three other ships were under weigh. The squadron was off Portland on the 6th March and off Plymouth Sound on the 7th where the *Burford* and the *St. Florentine* joined it. On the open sea, Admiral Pocock's flagship, the *Namur*, was in the lead, the other sails of the line and frigates forming two protective columns, one to starboard and one to larboard of the transports.

On 11th March, a sail was spotted by an alert lookout on the *Valiant* and the flagship gave permission for the *Valiant*, with the *Burford* and the *St Florentine* to give chase. The *Valiant*'s sails spread like wings as she ran before the wind and, with closing of the distance between her and her quarry, Captain Duncan instructed a boarding party to muster. Eventually, the *Valiant* and the stranger edged closer together, seamen taking in canvas and trimming yards before grapnels were swung and the boarding party jumped into action. Within minutes, the twenty gun French merchantman, the *St. Priest*, was taken. A prize crew from the *Burford* and the *St. Florentine* was put on board. The only other event of importance during the crossing of the Atlantic Ocean occurred on the 21st March when, in thick fog, contact was lost with five of the transports.

At five o'clock on the 20th April, forty-five days out from Spithead, the *Valiant* sighted Barbados and, at eight o'clock, she received orders

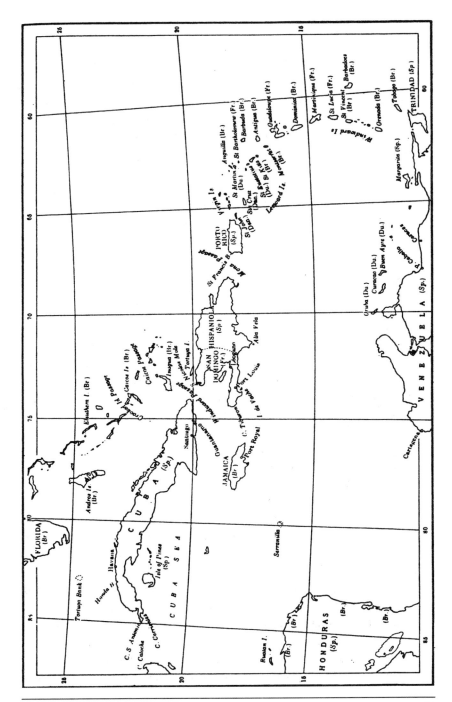

from the flagship, the *Namur*, to drop anchor. The fort's battery roared out a nineteen gun salute as a mark of respect for the Vice-Admiral and this was returned by the *Namur*. At Barbados, Pocock and Keppel learned that Admiral Rodney had captured the French-held island of Martinique. The loading of additional stores and victuals was completed on the 22nd April and, at six o'clock next morning, the Admiral signalled all ships to weigh anchor. In the meantime, the five missing transports arrived and joined the convoy.

On the *Valiant*, Captain Duncan gave the order to get the ship under weigh. The call, "Hands aloft! Loose tops'ls" made the rigging and shrouds come alive with swarming figures as the topmen ran aloft. The anchor was broken out, the capstan jerked and cranked steadily as dripping cable came inboard.

"Anchors aweigh, sir!" a voice shouted and the anchor was catted and made fast. All of this took time and it was noon before the convoy departed and a nineteen gun salute was fired by the fort's battery.

At six o'clock in the evening of the 26th April, the squadron and her accompanying transports dropped anchor off Cas des Navires in Martinique. The ships moved further in next morning and began the essential task of taking in water. Major General Robert Monckton was at Martinique with nine thousand troops already embarked on transports when Vice-Admiral Pocock's squadron arrived. Unfortunately, the transports were in such an unsavoury condition that disease had already caused some deaths amongst the soldiers. The embarkation of the troops had been poorly organised, regiments having chosen ships at random in which to embark and load their equipment. Following their experiences at Chesapeake Bay seven years previously, Keppel and Duncan knew the consequences of this, so time was spent checking the contents of individual vessels and making such adjustments as were necessary.

Whilst, as intended, the army corps had increased in strength to more than twelve thousand men, the expected increase in naval strength had not taken place. Rear-Admiral Rodney's sails of the line which should have joined Pocock's squadron had been distributed over a wide area to guard against a possible attack on Jamaica by French and Spanish squadrons thought to be cruising somewhere in the vicinity. Orders were despatched by fast craft instructing these ships to congregate at Cape St. Nicolas.

The force departed from Cas des Navires Bay on the 6th May and arrived off Cape St. Nicolas on the 17th. The naval squadron was increased in strength on the 25th May as vessels responded to the orders sent out by Admiral Pocock. It now consisted of twenty sails of the line, eleven lesser naval ships and about two hundred transports with eleven thousand troops and a siege train on board. Only the troops from America, under Lieutenant-General Amherst, had yet to join the force. On the 23rd May, it was found that of the 12,210 officers and men in Lord Albemarle's army corps, 1,289 were sick.

Rather than taking the longer route to Havana, involving sailing by the South side of Cuba, sweeping round the West end of the island and approaching Havana from the West, the plan was to steer along the North side of Cuba through the Old Bahama Channel which was rarely used. Whilst the channel was narrow and, in places, hazardous, it had the advantage of achieving surprise. The *Richmond* had been surveying the Channel for some weeks and three small vessels were now sent ahead of the fleet to take soundings and mark the route. On the 27th May, the huge fleet of about two hundred sailing ships left Cape St. Nicolas and bore away for Havana.

For the passage through the Channel, the transports were organised into seven divisions, each division accompanied by several men-of-war. The *Valiant* led the second division, comprising the troop transports with the 1st Brigade on board, two hospital ships and three artillery ships. By the 5th June, the Channel had been successfully cleared and, next day, the *Valiant's* lookout was the first man to sight land. Commodore Keppel was alerted. A boat was swung outboard and dropped and he settled himself in the sternsheets. Rowed to the flagship, he repaired on board to notify Admiral Pocock of the fleet's proximity to Havana. Shortly afterwards, ships were brought to about fifteen miles East of Havana and all captains repaired on board the flagship to receive their orders.

The Admiral explained how the entrance to the harbour, and much of Havana itself, was protected by the El Morro fortress, sited on the coast immediately to the East of the harbour entrance. Around its eastern and landward perimeter, the massive walls of the fortress were protected by a deep trench excavated into the *in situ* rock. An attack on Havana from the East would involve capturing the unprotected high ground of La Cabana to the South East of the fortress from where British guns could bombard the fortress, parts of the harbour and the city. Such a plan would mean Havana itself could not be taken until El Morro had first been reduced by siege operations. Alternatively, were the army to

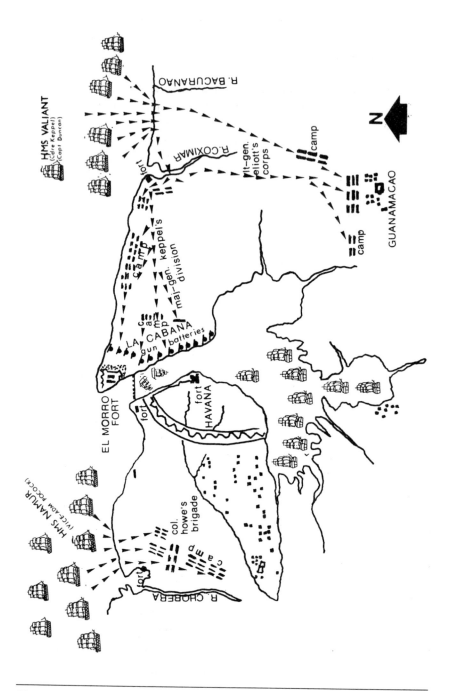

assault Havana from the North or West, it was thought troops would come under enfilade fire, either from El Morro fortress or from the guns of the Spanish ships in the harbour. Taking these factors into account, it had been decided to attack from the East. The troops would be brought ashore between the Bacuranao and Coximar rivers and Commodore Keppel would direct the landings. Vice-Admiral Pocock himself, with the men-of-war not required to cover the army's assault, and with the stores transports, would now proceed westwards towards Havana and Chorera. It was proposed that landings would take place next morning, the 7th June. Also, a diversionary attack would be made by marines, about four miles West of Havana, at Chorera.

Whilst Admiral Pocock's force weighed anchor and sailed westward, Commodore Keppel's squadron of seven sails of the line with four lesser ships and three bomb vessels took up positions offshore between the mouths of the Rivers Bacuranao and Coximar to cover the landings. The *Valiant* was the control centre for the operation, Captain Duncan having to ensure the commodore's orders were transmitted to the ships in the fleet.

At six o'clock in the morning of the 7th June, Duncan ordered a half blue, half yellow flag to be raised at the fore-topmasthead of the *Valiant*. This created a flurry of activity as flat-bottomed boats were swung overboard and dropped into the water from the men-of-war and the transports. Silently, sixteen oarsmen, a petty officer and a midshipman scrambled down the nettings to man each boat.

Now it was time for Duncan to order the hoisting of a half red, half white flag at the *Valiant's* fore-topmasthead. Each flat-bottomed boat was then rowed to its appointed troop transport and embarkation of the first wave of soldiers commenced. At the same time, the *Mercury*, the *Bonetta* and the *Basilisk* manoeuvred towards the mouth of the Bacuranao River while the *Richmond* and the *Trent*, with the seventy-four gun third rate sail of the line, HMS *Dragon*, under the command of Captain the Honourable August Hervey, took up positions off the landing area. The flat-bottomed boats displayed vanes of distinctive colours, designed to make it easier for those conveying soldiers of the same regiment to keep together. The boats were organised into "divisions", each having a naval officer in command whose duty it was to navigate his charges to their appointed landing areas.

When Duncan had a chequered red and white flag hoisted at the fore-topmasthead of the *Valiant* at nine o'clock, the boats set off for the shore.

Simultaneously, the guns of the ships lying off the River Bacuranao boomed out and the bombardment of the fort at the entrance to the river had begun. At the same time, the ships lying off the landing area commenced a bombardment of the wooded area inland of the shoreline. Leaving Captain Duncan to control operations from the *Valiant*, Commodore Keppel and General Lord Albemarle made for the shore in the *Valiant's* barge.

It was thirty minutes past ten o'clock when the first of the invading force approached land. There being a surf upon the shore, the midshipman in each of the boats dropped a grapnel so that, after the troops had disembarked, he would be sure to be able to haul his boat off again. As soon as the soldiers had landed, boats were rowed back with all haste to collect the next wave of troops. Just after three o'clock in the afternoon, by which time the weather had deteriorated, the first phase of the task allocated to Commodore Keppel and Captain Duncan had been completed, all of the troops having landed. Reports reaching the *Valiant* later in the day indicated that operations on land under Major-General William Keppel had proceeded satisfactorily, the Coximar River having been crossed and some units of the army having encamped for the night on its western side.

There was much activity over the next few days. The army's baggage had to be put ashore together with food supplies and light artillery pieces. Fifty of the *Valiant's* marines were involved clearing the enemy from La Cabana whilst others of the crew helped cut roadways through the woods to make it possible for cannons to be dragged up close to the El Morro fortress. Lieutenant-General Eliott's corps attacked and captured the village of Guanamacao to secure the army's southern flank. The Spaniards blocked the entrance to Havana harbour by sinking three men-of-war there. Although this prevented Admiral Pocock from entering and engaging enemy naval vessels, it contained the Spanish ships and permitted British naval forces to operate unchallenged in the waters off Havana. On the 11th June, in heavy rain, British troops completed the capture of La Cabana. If gun batteries could now be sited there, the siege and reduction of the El Morro fortress could begin. As planned, the diversionary attack went in at Chorera and this operation became increasingly important as the river was needed as a main source of water supply for the naval and military personnel operating in the East against El Morro.

A very gruelling few weeks followed. Six hundred sailors worked continuously for seventeen days building up the emplacements for the guns which would bombard El Morro and Havana. There was little soil cover to the rock in this area and earth-filled sandbags and fascines needed for the construction of the emplacements had to be conveyed by ship all the way from the Chorera bridgehead. A thousand sailors were needed to haul cannon and howitzers from the coast to the vicinity of El Morro in weather which alternated between periods of heavy rain and great heat. Drinkable water was in very short supply and had to be brought in casks from Chorera. Four howitzers were dragged into positions on La Cabana from where they could bombard the Spanish ships in the harbour. During the whole of this period, the British force was subjected to incessant fire from the guns of the Spanish men-of-war in the harbour at Havana and from the guns of the El Morro fortress.

By the 1st July, work on the emplacements had been completed and cannons and guns were in position. The bombardment of El Morro started, both from the land-based batteries and from the guns of the *Dragon*, the *Cambridge*, the *Marlborough* and the *Stirling Castle*. The enemy's response was a vigorous one and much damage was done to the masts, sails and rigging of the four ships which, in addition, lost forty-four officers and men killed and one hundred and forty-eight wounded. The ships' guns had difficulty projecting shot and shells into the fortress because of the height of its perimeter walls but they did succeed in diverting the enemy's fire from the troops on La Cabana. After twenty-four hours, the landward batteries had caused some damage to the wall of El Morro. However, on the 2nd July, a lack of rain over the preceding days and continuous firing was causing the guns and the fascines to become hot. Next day, the fascines burst into flames. There was insufficient water nearby to extinguish the fires and all the hard work undertaken since the beginning of the month was lost.

Captain Duncan and his crew were involved in all aspects of this work in support of the army. Duncan became increasingly concerned about the health of his men. Shortage of water, malaria and dysentery caused more casualties than the enemy's gunfire. Fever was taking its toll and whilst this killed some men in a few hours, it took weeks before others died, their putrifying bodies riddled with disease. One member of the crew of the *Valiant* was now dying each day. At one time, five thousand soldiers and three thousand sailors were sick. Lieutenant-General Eliott's division had to abandon Guanamacao and merge with the units on La Cabana as only four hundred out of two thousand five hundred of his soldiers were fit for duty. Commodore Keppel was frequently unwell and even Duncan's strong constitution protested at times, making him ache and feel lethargic.

Reconstruction of the gun emplacements was a matter of prime importance. A large party from the *Valiant*, with Duncan frequently in their midst providing encouragement and help, completed the emplacement works for eight thirty-two pounder guns, referred to thereafter as "the *Valiant's* battery". It took five hundred sailors and one thousand five hundred slave labourers until the 17th July to completely reconstruct the earlier gun emplacements lost in the fire.

A most intense and continuous bombardment of the fortress recommenced, hundreds of rounds of shell and shot being projected into it every day. Individual guns were firing about one hundred and fifty times over a period of sixteen hours. For the British, it was a battle not only against the Spaniards but against disease and sickness resulting from the very hot days and the damp nights, exacerbated by the intense physical work demanded of every man each day under a pitiless June sun. If the Spaniards could hold out long enough, the British would be forced to withdraw because of the increasing death toll from tropical diseases.

By the middle of July, the El Morro fortress had suffered greatly and the next phase of the operation could commence. The major obstacle to be overcome by Major-General Keppel's assault troops was the ditch, about twenty metres deep in places and thirty metres wide, which extended around the fortress on its landward sides. The bank sloping down from the fort was of solid rock, so approach trenches could not be dug. However, one narrow ridge of unexcavated rock was found at the seaward end of the trench, this having been left in order to prevent the trench from being inundated by the sea. The ridge was only wide enough for men to walk in single file but it did give access to the base of the wall of the fortress.

Two actions were now taken. To help the engineers, the crews of the various ships were combed to find men who had worked in the Cornish mines as, indeed, had some of the crew of the *Valiant*. After a dangerous rush along the ridge to the wall of the fortress, during which four men were killed by small arms fire, mining work was started preparatory to laying charges and blowing a hole in the wall. At the same time, further mines were placed in order to cause collapse of the side slopes of the trench in the hope that the resultant debris would widen the ridge and give easier access to the wall of the fortress for the assaulting troops. Spanish units made several attacks on the sappers and miners but, on every occasion, they were beaten back. By the 29th July, the charges had been placed and all was ready for the attack on El Morro.

The final assault was set to take place on the 30th July. Very early in the morning of that day, miners working in the ditch were showered with musket fire and grape shot from several light Spanish craft which had moved round the northern, seaward, side of the fortress. Commodore Keppel ordered Captain Duncan to take several boatloads of armed men from the *Valiant* and deal with them. However, by the time the *Valiant*'s boats arrived in the area, the enemy had departed, having themselves come under heavy fire from the troops giving cover to the miners. Captain Duncan returned to the *Valiant* but, at ten o'clock the next morning he was again despatched in command of the armed boats, this time to join the *Alcide* which was anchored near El Morro. Whilst the commodore had failed to receive permission from his brother, Major-General Keppel, for the employment of sailors in the assault on El Morro he had, nevertheless, instructed Duncan to sieze any opportunity to be of service to the army.

At two o'clock in the afternoon of the 30th July, the mines were sprung. Although one of the explosions failed to widen the access ridge to the fortress, the wall of El Morro itself had been breached and the order to attack was given. Men of the Royal Regiment, the 90th Regiment and the 35th Regiment, under the command of Colonel James Stuart, filed quickly along the ridge, scrambled up the rough slope leading to El Morro and were through the hole in the wall before encountering the enemy. Captain Duncan and his party had come ashore and they raced across the narrow ridge in single file, clambered up the rough slope and joined in the melee in the fortress.

The hand-to-hand fighting was fierce. By the time the British had lost thirty-two officers and men killed and wounded and the Spanish one hundred and sixty-seven, the remaining three hundred and twenty-six defenders of El Morro surrendered. A further two hundred and thirteen were killed or were drowned attempting to escape by boat to Havana.

For several hours after the capture of El Morro, it and its British captors came under heavy bombardment from one hundred cannons of the Spanish men-of-war in the harbour and from their land-based batteries. More arduous work was now necessary, including the construction of additional gun emplacements and the moving of artillery and thirty-five pieces of cannon to La Cabana, from where fire could be concentrated on Havana and on the ships in the harbour. Rather belatedly, the first of the troops from America arrived and joined those in the bridgehead to the West of Havana. Lord Albemarle now gave the Spanish governor, Don Juan de Prado, the opportunity to surrender in order to prevent further casualties. However, before his aide-de-camp could return to the British lines with a rejection of the offer, the Spanish had recommenced firing.

On the 10th August, the *Valiant* sailed westwards and anchored off the mouth of the River Chorera as part of the build up of forces for an attack against the West walls of the city. As well as being bombarded by British batteries on La Cabana in the East, there were now forty cannon, five howitzers and ten mortars located to the West of Havana. A heavy bombardment of Havana and adjacent forts took place on the 11th August. Next day, Don Juan de Prado realised his position was untenable. Terms of capitulation were agreed and British troops occupied the city on the 14th. One thousand Spanish troops and twelve hundred sailors were taken prisoner.

Captain Duncan was given the task of taking possession of the Spanish naval vessels in the harbour at Havana. This involved organising his officers and crew to accept the surrender of five seventy gun and four sixty gun sail of the line lying at anchor, three ships lying on the bottom of the entrance channel and two ships on the stocks. These prizes constituted one fifth of the entire Spanish navy. The harbour entrance had to be cleared to permit the British ships to enter and refit. The *Valiant* was in a poor state, her pumps going continuously to keep out the water and she was badly in need of careening.

The operation had been a great success. However, eight hundred seamen and five hundred marines had died, of whom eighty-six were killed during the siege of El Morro. Sickness continued after the surrender of Havana and, on the 9th October, two thousand six hundred and seventy-three seamen and six hundred marines were unfit for duty, some of them likely to die rather than to recover. Army losses in the campaign were five hundred and sixty officers and men killed or died of wounds and four thousand seven hundred and eight died of sickness. Seamen who remained on board ship and had no contact with those on shore tended to be healthier than their fellows working with the army. Those soldiers who were required to undertake hard physical work on the higher, drier and shadier ground of La Canaba, largely feeding on salt food and having a long way to walk to replenish their poor quality water supplies, fared better than those soldiers stationed in more open country and whose tasks were less onerous.

Many of those who survived the rigours of the campaign suffered from poor health for the remainder of their lives. The Earl of Albemarle was never again a fit man and Captain Duncan's constitution was so affected that further service in the West Indies was inadvisable.

The total prize money was vast. At £736,000 it represented about £130,000,000 at today's value, and was distributed as shown on the following page.

On the 12 October, Captain Duncan in the *Valiant*, together with six other sails of the line and several frigates, left Havana for Port Royal in Jamaica. During the voyage they intercepted and captured a convoy of thirteen Frenchmen laden with coffee, indigo and sugar. The *Valiant's* pumps were constantly working to deal with very bad leaks but she did manage to reach Port Royal on the 3rd November. In January 1763, Commodore Keppel was promoted to the rank of Rear-Admiral and appointed to replace Vice-Admiral Pocock who had returned to England. All the Spanish prize ships were sent back to England under the command of Captain Arbuthnot in the *Orford*, with five other sails of the line and a number of frigates in attendance.

On the 10th February 1763, a peace treaty was signed marking the end of what became known as the Seven Years' War. It saw Great Britain at the height of her imperial achievement. She was undisputed master of America and India and had achieved supremacy on the seas. France and Spain had been decisively defeated, the former relinquishing her interests in Canada, Nova Scotia, Cape Breton, the islands of the St. Lawrence River, the valley of the Ohio and all the territory East of the Mississippi except New Orleans. Havana was restored to Spain in exchange for Florida which became British. On the 6th July 1763, the last British troops departed from the city. Thereafter, Cuba was once again under the government of Carlos III of Spain. There were those who thought the exchange of strategically-important Havana for the then desolate and unproductive Florida was a bad deal.

Captain Adam Duncan was one of forty-two captains serving in Vice-Admiral Pocock's fleet. Each one played an important part in the operations which resulted in the capture of Havana. Duncan would expect no greater credit than any of his colleagues but he was favoured through having worked closely with Commodore Keppel and, as a result, having substantial responsibility for the success of the landing of the main body of the assault troops on the 7th June. He and his men from the *Valiant* also played major parts in the construction of the road leading to El Morro, in hauling cannon from the coast to emplacements near the fortress, in the building of the gun emplacements and in providing the crew for what became known as "the *Valiant*'s battery".

Professionally, he had accumulated yet more experience in the conduct of joint operations with the army. He was able to put into practice lessons learned the hard way in America and at the Isle of Aix which, in Cuba, led to the smooth disembarkation of the troops and their successful landing on the beach between the Bacuranao and Coximar rivers. Over the years, the *Valiant* had become his home and the crew was his family. In the arduous climatic conditions under which they all lived, worked and suffered sickness and disease, he showed a constant regard for the welfare of his officers and men. He took every opportunity to improve their lot, whether it was in the provision of fresh food and vegetables or in their safety under fire.

He was never heard to talk badly of anyone and he was loathe to condemn a subordinate unless he had failed in his duties. Even under

	Amount of Prize Money Received	Present Day Equivalent
To Vice-Admiral Pocock	£122,000	£21,500,000
To Lt-Gen Lord Albemarle	£122,000	£21,500,000
To Commodore Keppel and Lt-Gen Eliott	£24,000	£4,200,000
To Captains, R.N.	£1,600	£280,000
To Petty Officers	£17	£3,000
To Soldiers	£4	£700
To Sailors	£3.75	£660

the unpleasant conditions prevailing in the ship and on shore in Cuba, he was never heard to complain but, rather, he was always amiable and cheerful. When men transgressed, they knew they could rely on him to judge them fairly and firmly. They knew too that, like themselves, he lived frugally.

It was his policy to take his officers into his confidence, to give them all available information on the task and, when responsibility had been delegated, to leave them to get on with the job. In the case of the men, he strived constantly to improve their efficiency by proper training and exercise. It was widely known he was a good seaman who ran an efficient ship. The *Valiant's* boats could be let down without swamping even although the speed of the *Valiant* was never reduced.

The *Valiant* remained on station in the West Indies until the 8th May 1864 when she left Port Royal, arriving in England on the 26th June. She was paid off and Captain Adam Duncan, now almost thirty-three years of age, was placed on the Unemployed List on half pay which was the fate of most of his naval colleagues in times of peace.

Chapter 8 • INTERLUDE

MANY YEARS SPENT IN DAMP CONDITIONS on board ship and, in particular, the last two when he had been subjected to the rigours of a tropical climate, left Duncan feeling lethargic and fatigued for many months after his return to Britain. He was advised his constitution would not stand further service in the tropics. Of necessity, therefore, his first two years on the Unemployed List were spent recuperating, and he chose to do so in Bath and Cheltenham.

He had always worried about money and financial security. The prize money from the expedition to Havana was a lump sum, equivalent to six years of a captain's salary, and he also received half pay (about seven shillings per day) whilst on the Unemployed List. This was a fortune when compared with the wages of a ploughman at that time which was about one pound eight shillings per year plus board and lodgings, or a servant girl who earned about one pound per year plus two pairs of shoes.

The war was succeeded by a serious economic slump and there were violent disputes and unrest in some towns and cities. In country areas, there were food riots when bad harvests made life difficult for the poorer people as the prices of essential foodstuffs rose. Petty crime was common, particularly against property. In 1765, troops had to be called in when silk weavers in London rioted, believing that preference was being given to silks imported from France. The under-classes were stirring as the struggle for a more equitable distribution of wealth got under way.

As the years passed, changes for the better did occur, with improvements in the layout of some cities and towns. Duncan himself appreciated this when he visited the New Town in Edinburgh. Neat rows of new houses were springing up and the concept of the pleasant city square was becoming fashionable. In London, sewers and water mains were being laid and some streets were being cobbled and paved for the first time. There were real rises in the standards of living, certainly for the middle and upper classes.

Society was changing, albeit slowly, and Duncan wondered how this would affect the navy in the years ahead. The figures released by the Admiralty for the war which had just ended were a cause for some concern. During the Seven Years' War, the navy had employed 184,893 seamen and marines of whom only 1,512 had been killed in action or as a result of accidents. However, by the end of the war only 49,673 remained on the roll which meant that 133,708 (or 72% of the total employed) had either died from disease or had deserted the service. There were clearly problems associated with the appalling conditions in which men of the lower deck were expected to live and work.

In 1767, Captain Duncan moved North to his home at Lundie and he was there when his father died in 1771. The estate passed to the captain's elder brother, Major Alexander Duncan, now retired from the army after more than twenty years service. Their only other brother, John, had died some years previously whilst serving in China. As Alexander had not yet married, Adam and his three youngest sisters, Margaret, Helen and Isobella, with their mother, continued to live in Lundie Castle.

Alexander had purchased his commission in the Fifty-Fifth Regiment of Foot which had been raised in the neighbourhood of Stirling at the time of the Jacobite rebellion in 1745. Its introduction to war had been somewhat traumatic. When faced with a charge by Highlanders of Lord George Murray's Jacobite Army at Falkirk on the 17th January 1746, the bulk of the regiment's recently-recruited men fled the field. Alexander and some of his brother officers stood firm and came out of the battle unscathed. There followed periods of service with the regiment in Flanders, Ireland and Great Britain.

The Fifty-Fifth, under the command of Colonel Lord Howe, was one of three regiments which sailed for Canada in June 1757 to join Major-General Abercromby's division at Halifax, Nova Scotia, preparing for an attack on the French garrison at Louisburg. In 1758, the regiment was despatched, as part of General Abercromby's fifteen thousand strong force, to attack the French-held garrison of Ticonderoga on Lake George, out of which the Hudson River flowed. It was impressive country, the Appalachians lying to the East and the Adirondack Mountains to the West. In an early skirmish with the enemy, the Fifty-Fifth's commanding officer, Lord Howe, was killed. His death deeply affected the men of the regiment for he was courageous, kind, generous and possessed of an engaging personality. He was, in effect, the life and soul of the regiment. It was under such a man that Alexander Duncan received his military training.

After peace was made with the French in 1763, Alexander commanded six companies of his regiment charged with protecting settlements in Ontario from relentless harassing by Indians, irritated by the encroachment of settlers on to their lands. For two years his soldiers manned isolated outposts across the countryside. Alexander was a very sound regimental officer, highly thought of by his fellow officers and by his men. He had a good sense of humour and invariably acted in a friendly, fair but firm way in all matters. He was held in awe by his young officers and, like his brother, was looked upon as a father-figure by his men. He was studious and, wherever he went, he was surrounded by books on a wide range of subjects which his young officers were encouraged to borrow. To relieve the monotony when not on active service, he ran gardening and farming courses for his men.

In 1771, news of Rear-Admiral Keppel's promotion to Vice-Admiral gave Adam Duncan much pleasure. In the years which followed and despite the long and tedious journeys involved, he made regular visits to the Admiralty in London in the hope their Lordships would be enticed to give him a ship. Nothing ever transpired as a result of these trips and so, in 1774, he went off to Italy for a holiday, whilst there staying with his aunt, Lady Mary Duncan, the wife of Sir William Duncan, Physician Extraordinary to King George the Second. Adam's eldest sister, Katherine, who had married James Haldane of Airthrey in 1762, died during 1774.

During his years at home in Scotland, Captain Duncan was not lacking in company or in invitations to the many country houses where his close, and distant, relatives resided. Through his mother, he was related to the Haldanes of Gleneagles; through his paternal grandmother to the Murrays of Ochtertyre and through his paternal great grandmother to the Drummonds of Megginch. It was at one such country house that he met the lady who, in 1777, became his wife. She was Henrietta Dundas, daughter of the Right Honourable Robert Dundas of Arniston, Lord President of the Court of Session.

At the time of his marriage, Duncan was forty-six years of age and thirteen years had passed since his last naval appointment. However, he had never lost hope of being given a ship again. 1776 brought the Declaration of American Independence and the likelihood of an expansion of the fleet. As his wife and he celebrated the birth of their first child, Jane, in 1778, they received news at their new home in Edinburgh that Vice-Admiral Keppel had been promoted to the rank of Admiral. Shortly afterwards, Captain Duncan was ordered to take command of HMS *Suffolk* which he proceeded to do on the 16th May.

Chapter 9 • RODNEY'S MOONLIGHT BATTLE

IN 1778, NORTH AMERICA WAS THE SCENE of a military struggle between a British army of fifty thousand men and local independence fighters in the colony. As a result of France entering into commercial treaties with the colonists, war between France and Britain became inevitable. This time, having offended her usual allies, Britain was forced to fight alone. Also, there was no land war on the continent and, as a consequence, France was able to concentrate all of her efforts on the naval conflict.

In the days and weeks which followed Captain Duncan assuming command of the *Suffolk* (a seventy-four gun sail of the line fitting out at Chatham) the condition into which the navy had fallen during his enforced absence became depressingly obvious. Many of the ships were in very poor condition, unseasoned timber having been used in those built during the Seven Years' War. They had rotted quite badly in the intervening thirteen years and it was thought only six ships out of a total of thirty-five in the Channel Fleet were thoroughly seaworthy. Against this, it was known the French had been improving their naval dockyards and had built better designed and faster sails of the line of which they now had eighty. French naval officers were well educated and there was a proper system of conscription which provided seamen for the French navy on a regular basis.

In other respects too, Duncan found the years of peace had been detrimental to efficiency. By the end of the Seven Years' War, scurvy had almost been eliminated from the navy through a realisation of the importance of fruit and fresh vegetables in the men's diet. Unfortunately, the situation was again as bad as ever. Also, he was aware that relationships between officers and men had deteriorated in some ships because of the extent to which some officers abused their powers by having men beaten for trivial offences and by encouraging the liberal use of the lash and the ropes-end.

For this and other reasons, fewer men were coming forward as volunteers and, consequently, larger numbers had to be pressed into service. Many of the pressed men were thoroughly experienced seamen taken from the merchant fleet whilst others were landsmen some of whom arrived in filthy clothing which inevitably resulted in an increase in sickness and fevers. Many felt aggrieved as pay had not been increased since the time of Cromwell and, per month, was still only twenty four shillings for an Able Bodied Seamen and nineteen shillings for an Ordinary Seamen. Matters were made worse because this was only a quarter of the money that could be earned on a merchantman and, in any event, pay was often years in arrears which meant seamen's families were living in poverty and only surviving with the help of parish relief.

Captain Duncan had the *Suffolk* in an operational condition by the end of August 1778 and, after a period of duty with coastal convoys, she joined Admiral Augustus Keppel's Channel Fleet until the end of October. As was his custom, he did everything in his power to make the lives of his crew as comfortable as possible within the retrictions imposed by the ship.

Captain Duncan was then ordered to command the *Monarch*, a seventy-four gun sail of the line, and was set the task of getting her and her crew to a high level of efficiency as soon as possible. There had been several improvements in gunnery since his last period of active service and the gun crews had to be practised in these. One was the carronade, invented by Mr. Gascoigne of the Carron Ironworks. This was a shorter and lighter version of the carriage gun which fired a heavier than normal projectile but over a shorter distance. It recoiled on a slide and could be manned by fewer men. Another improvement in gunnery increased the rate of firing to two rounds every three minutes and permitted firing obliquely.

In June of 1779, by which time Captain Duncan had brought the *Monarch*'s crew up to standard in both seamanship and gunnery, Spain had joined in the war on the side of France. She did so in order to regain sovereignty over Gibraltar and Minorca and also because her government harboured an ambition to invade the mainland of Great Britain. To achieve the latter, she would require to secure a major victory over Britain's Channel Fleet, command of which had been given to Admiral Sir Charles Hardy, now virtually an invalid.

The *Monarch*, with the other thirty-four ships of Hardy's Fleet, had been cruising in the English Channel since the 16th June. As the month drew to a close, the British government became increasingly alarmed at the build-up of naval and military forces on the French coast. Under the command of Marechal De Vaux, fifty thousand French troops were known to have assembled at Le Havre and St. Malo preparatory to embarking on four hundred transport ships already anchored there. The army's objective was the capture of the Isle of Wight whilst the combined French and Spanish fleet of fifty sails of the line under Admiral d'Orvilliers had the task of securing Spithead as its anchorage. As it crossed the channel, the convoy of troop-carrying transports was to be given protection by sixteen sails of the line under the Spanish Admiral de Cordova.

In England, there was near-panic amongst the general public. On the 9th July, a Royal Proclamation ordered the interception of the combined French and Spanish Fleet and it also required all horses and cattle to be removed from coastal areas. To prevent the entry of foreign ships, booms were placed across the entrance to Plymouth Harbour. There was concern for convoys of heavily-laden merchantmen heading home to England, one from Jamaica consisting of two hundred ships, another from the Leeward Islands and eight East Indiamen.

On the 16th August, the combined fleet of sixty-six sail of the line was off Plymouth having coincidentally missed making contact with Admiral Hardy's squadrons. Admiral d'Orvilliers was notified when already at sea of a change in the site of the landings from the Isle of Wight to Cornwall, a ridiculous location since no suitable anchorage existed there for his massive fleet and also because, from a military point of view, it was too remote to be of much use to an invading army. Whilst awaiting a reply from his government to his protest at the change in the invasion plan, a strong easterly wind blew up and this carried the combined fleet out of the English Channel. From intelligence reports, Admiral d'Orvilliers understood the British fleet was cruising about sixty miles South West of the Scilly Isles. As increasing numbers of his seamen were becoming ill and as provisions were running low, he decided to seek out and bring the British fleet to battle at the earliest possible moment.

On the 29th August, the *Monarch* was heading eastwards in the English Channel with the other thirty-seven men-of-war in Admiral Hardy's command when the combined fleet of sixty-six sails of the line was sighted. The two fleets met on the 1st September some miles from Eddystone but, given the disparity in strength, Hardy avoided battle and sought refuge at Spithead where he anchored on the 3rd September. For the next ten days, the combined fleet dominated the English Channel.

It was the 14th September before it retired to Brest. Eventually, the Spanish ships were recalled to Spain and, thereafter, priority was given to blockading British-held Gibraltar and to creating maximum disruption to British naval forces in American waters, Asia and the West Indies. That Great Britain was spared invasion was due more to the ineptitude of her enemies than to any commendable action of her own.

Captain Duncan was furious at having been associated with a British squadron which had deliberately avoided action with the enemy. To him, it was not an adequate excuse that the fleets had varied so greatly in numbers. Whether or not he was right to take this view cannot be known but it was a situation with which, when an admiral, he was to be faced later in his career. It was clear to him, and to many others that, inexcusably, Britain had been unprepared for the war in which she was now engaged. It was foreseeable months beforehand that Spain would enter the war. From a purely naval point of view, for the British Channel fleet not to have blockaded the French fleet in Brest before its strength was augmented by the arrival of the Spanish ships, was a grave error. Even as he waited at Spithead in the early days of September, Duncan could not understand why Hardy's squadrons were not pursuing the homeward bound Spanish fleet after its departure from Brest. Over the years, Duncan had gathered much experience in joint operations with the army, and in chasing and boarding enemy privateers and merchantmen but, as a senior captain now forty-eight years of age, he had never taken part in a major sea battle. It was a deficiency he hoped would be rectified.

Since the entry of Spain into the war, Gibraltar had been blockaded by sixteen of her men-of-war operating out of Cadiz and Algeciras. These ships intercepted and siezed all vessels trying to enter the Rock. The British Mediterranean Squadron, comprising a sixty gun sail of the line, three frigates and a sloop, was too weak to challenge the Spanish blockade. Supplies of all kinds were running very low in Gibraltar and its early relief was becoming a matter of some urgency.

On the 29th December, the *Monarch*, with Captain Duncan in command, departed from Plymouth along with another twenty-one sails of the line, fourteen frigates, some lesser naval vessels and a huge fleet of transports carrying troops, stores, victuals, ordnance and general merchandise, all under the command of sixty-two year old Admiral Rodney whose object was to break the blockade of Gibraltar. By the 8th

January 1780, when the fleet was about three hundred miles West of Cape Finisterre, twenty-two sail were seen. With the other ships in Rodney's squadron, the *Monarch* gave chase and played a full part in the boarding and capture of the Spanish men-of-war, the *Guipuscoana* of sixty-four guns (taken into the Royal Navy and re-named the *Prince William*), the *San Carlos*, the *San Rafael*, the *San Bruno*, the *Santa Teresa*, the *San Fermin* and the *San Vincente*. But also taken as prizes were fifteen merchantmen, twelve laden with provisions. A British crew was placed on board the *Guipuscoana* which was ordered off to give protection to a convoy consisting of the captured Spanish provision ships now diverted to Gibraltar.

Eight days later, whilst passing Cape St. Vincent at one o'clock in the afternoon of the 16th January 1780, a signal was passed to Admiral Rodney, who at the time was confined to his cabin suffering from gout, informing him that sails had been observed in the South East. He gave orders for the squadron to prepare for battle, to bear down on the sails with all speed and for his ships to form line abreast. On seeing Rodney's signal on the flagship, Captain Duncan ordered, "Beat to quarters! Clear ship for action!"

The crew had been well-trained and there was an instant flurry of activity as the boatswain's mates went through the ship, shouting to the men to go to quarters. The decks were sanded, water was poured over the hammock rolls, sails, boom and ship's boats. Nettings were emplaced over the upper decks to catch rigging and men who might fall from above. Grapnels were made ready and boarding parties assembled after collecting cutlasses, axes and pikes. Men took up their positions by the portlids, clutching the lanyard that would trice it up and allow the guns to be run out. With the yards hard braced and the wheel over, the *Monarch* struggled round to larboard to come into line abreast.

There was the constant flap and thunder of sail as the *Monarch* bore down on the distant ship. As her bow dipped, the forecastle was drenched with showers of spray. Captain Duncan ordered the t'gallants and royals on her in an effort to get more speed. This sent men swarming up the ratlines on either beam. Within two hours, it was realised the quarry being chased was a Spanish squadron comprising eleven sails of the line and two twenty-six gun frigates.

At about three o'clock in the afternoon, with a westerly wind blowing, the enemy was seen to form line of battle on the starboard tack, their heads directed southwards towards the shelter of Cadiz. Admiral Rodney now ordered, "General Chase! To Leeward! In rotation," meaning that the first one of his ships to contact the enemy should engage the last sail of the enemy's line, those ships following then passing to the leeward of the first and attacking the next unengaged enemy ship towards the van.

Half an hour later, Duncan could see that ships in the van of the British squadron were rapidly bearing down on those at the rear of the Spanish squadron. At four o'clock, the signal for battle was made and, within minutes, the sound of gunfire was heard as the four leading British men-of-war engaged the enemy. Sailing under full canvas, the *Monarch* continued to bear down on the Spanish squadron and, at forty minutes past four o'clock, all on board heard a great explosion as one of the seventy gun Spanish ships, the *Santo Domingo*, blew up. The sight from the *Monarch* was spectacular, flames shooting skywards from the stricken vessel and explosion after explosion resounding across the water. The *Santo Domingo* went down with all hands.

As it was winter, daylight was lost shortly afterwards. However, there was a full moon that night and, although the weather conditions deteriorated as time went on, the chase continued. In the eerie light of the moon, another Spanish sail of the line struck its colours during the early evening.

By nine o'clock, the *Monarch* came under fire from guns sited in the sterns of three seventy gun Spanish ships, the *San Augustin*, the *Monarca* and the *San Julian*.

"Brail the fores'l and mains'l up to the yards," Duncan ordered, endeavouring to ensure the lower sails would neither impair his vision nor ignite. He wanted to avoid firing until he was close to the enemy, on their leeward side and able to employ a maximum number of guns. As it took about ten minutes to run out the guns, he ordered in good time, "Open gun ports! Run out the guns!"

At thirty minutes past nine o'clock, Captain Duncan gave the order, "Fire!" Flashes and smoke were emitted from the *Monarch*'s guns. She was now close to, and under fire from, the three Spanish sail of the line. Duncan had trained his gun crews well and their rate of firing was considerably higher than was being achieved by the Spaniards who, in any event, disliked doing battle at such close quarters. On the *Monarch*'s gun decks, flintlocks were repeatedly cocked, the firing lanyards were constantly being pulled and, over and over again, guns boomed and then recoiled violently. In the eerie light of the full moon, the small, shadowy figures of the powder boys could be seen rushing between the gun decks and the magazine, clutching wooden cylinders with close-fitting lids in which powder cartridges for the guns were being carried. In the dark, Duncan had to ensure he did not come too close to an enemy ship in case their yards locked. He also made sure he was not fighting with too much sail since this could have been dangerous. The topsails alone were quite enough to give him complete control of the ship.

A shot from one of the Spanish ships struck the *Monarch* forward of the quarterdeck. Overlying netting was ripped. Almost immediately afterwards, another shot damaged the foretop mast, the canvas and rigging. There were screams and moans from men seen to stagger and collapse on to the deck. The *Monarch*'s own guns roared as shot was projected uninterruptedly into the enemy ships close by. Successive salvos from the enemy shredded much of the *Monarch*'s sails whilst others ripped the shrouds and the top of the foretopgallant mast. There was a sickening judder as a shot penetrated the *Monarch*'s hull.

The battle raged for two hours and, before midnight, the *San Augustin* struck her colours and indicated her intention to surrender to the *Monarch*. At about this time, Admiral Rodney, in the Sandwich, came to the *Monarch*'s assistance. After firing one broadside at the *Monarca* she surrendered, having earlier suffered much damage from the *Monarch*'s guns. However, the *St. Julian* managed to slip away without being intercepted.

Duncan ordered a boat to be made ready to repair to the *San Augustin* but the weather worsened and the *Monarch*'s boat could not be launched. In these conditions and in the confusion of the battle, the *San Augustin* escaped and eventually managed to reach the safety of Cadiz. The ships of Rodney's fleet continued to do battle until two hours after midnight by which time six of the enemy sails of the line had surrendered with their commander, Admiral Don Juan de Langara. Of the remaining five ships, the *Santo Domingo* had blown up and four others, including the *San Augustin* had escaped.

During the battle, the *Monarch* had lost three men killed and twenty-six men wounded, the latter attended to by the ship's surgeon who operated in the midshipmen's berth. When amputations were required, the patient was given rum designed to deadened the pain and he was then strapped to the table in the berth. When the offending leg or arm had been severed, the stump was cauterised with hot tar and the severed limb thrown into the tub used for holding unwanted appendages.

The very stormy weather continued for the remainder of that night and for the whole of the next day. Many ships of Rodney's squadron, including the *Monarch*, were in some danger from the shoals of San Lucar and it took a high degree of skill in seamanship before all vessels were again in deep waters. Because of the bad weather and unfavourable currents, the *Monarch* did not anchor at Gibraltar until the 26th January. The blockade had been successfully broken. Although the Spanish Admiral de Cordova had twenty four sails of the line lying at anchor in Cadiz Bay, he did not at any time attempt to intercept Admiral Rodney's squadron. Following repairs to her rigging and hull, the *Monarch* departed from Gibraltar on the 13th February 1780 and, with other ships of the Channel fleet, escorted the prizes back to England.

Captain Duncan, his wife and their three young children, Jane, Alexander and William now made their home in Gosport. The Duncans were exceedingly hospitable and there was a constant stream of naval officers visiting and being entertained at their residence. The captain was able to spend some time with his wife and family whilst the *Monarch* was being refitted and, later, between cruises with the Channel Fleet. However, when the *Monarch* was ordered to the West Indies in September 1781, he was persuaded by the medical officer to decline tropical service.

The year 1782 saw Duncan's great friend, Admiral the Honourable Augustus Keppel raised to the peerage as Viscount Keppel. It was March before Duncan was appointed captain of the second rate, ninety gun, sail of the line, HMS *Blenheim*, the largest ship he had so far commanded. Gibraltar was again under blockade, having received neither reinforcements nor supplies since April 1781. The *Blenheim* was ordered to join Admiral Howe's Channel Fleet along with thirty-three other sails of the line, twelve lesser naval vessels and one hundred and thirty-seven transports and supply ships gathering at Spithead. However, a tragedy occurred prior to the departure of the expedition. Whilst undergoing repairs, the one hundred gun sail of the line, the *Royal George*, sank carrying with her to the sea bed Rear-Admiral Kempenfelt and nine hundred others, including women and children.

It was the 11th September 1782 before Howe's expedition left Spithead. Inevitably, the progress of such a large convoy was slow but the quality of the seamanship exhibited by all of the participants was commendable. Despite fierce gales, all one hundred and eighty-three ships were accounted for when the storms abated, no significant scattering having taken place. An intelligence report brought to Admiral Howe on the 10th October as the convoy approached Gibraltar told of a combined French and Spanish fleet comprising forty-eight sails of the line lying at anchor at Algeciras, only four miles across the water from Gibraltar.

On the 10th October, Captain Duncan was summoned to a conference attended by the other captains and flag officers in the fleet at which Admiral Howe revealed his proposed tactics and issued his orders. For the passage through the Straits of Gibraltar, the transport and supply ships were to take the lead, followed by the men-of-war organised in three squadrons, one squadron in the van, one squadron in the centre commanded personally by Admiral Howe and one squadron bringing up the rear. Captain Duncan in the *Blenheim* was to lead the larboard column of the Admiral's squadron.

There was a westerly wind blowing as the first of the convoy of transports entered the Straits at noon on the 11th October and by six o'clock they were off the mouth of the Bay of Gibraltar. Misunderstanding their orders, the transports sailed past the entrance to the bay and were carried off to the East. For their protection, Admiral Howe now had no choice but to follow them with his three squadrons. On the 13th, the transports, with their accompanying naval ships, were anchored fifty miles to the East of Gibraltar. As the sun was setting, the combined fleet was observed on the horizon. Howe formed up his naval squadrons and headed South during the night, his main interest being that the transport ships should arrive safely in Gibraltar rather than that he should become involved in a major sea battle. From the mastheads of his ships next morning, the enemy's combined fleet was still visible about twelve miles away. By the 15th October, the wind was set fair for the convoy to reach Gibraltar and by the 18th all of the transports had anchored there.

The combined fleet was observed by Admiral Howe's squadrons on the morning of the 19th October but it was the evening of the 20th October before contact was made. Not wishing to fight within the confines of the Straits, Howe ordered his squadrons westwards into more open waters where he formed line of battle off Cape Spartel. The enemy fleet followed him and there was an exchange of fire for several hours during which, in the *Blenheim*, two men were killed and three men were wounded. Eventually, the combined fleet withdrew and Admiral Howe's squadron set sail for England, arriving at Spithead on the 14th November 1782. The *Blenheim* was ordered to the West Indies and, again, Captain Duncan had to decline the posting on health grounds.

On the 1st April 1783 and now in his fifty-second year, Duncan took command of HMS *Edgar*, the guardship at Portsmouth. He was able to live at home with his wife and their five young children, Jane, Alexander, William, Henrietta and Adamina, all of whom were under the age of six. These were golden years for the happy parents and for their young family, surrounded as they were by many friends in this most pleasant part of England.

With the signing of the Peace of Versailles in 1783, the war was at an end and, at that time, some matters came to Duncan's notice which did not augur well for naval discipline in the future. There was a delay in releasing many men from their ships following the cessation of hostilities and, as a consequence, serious disturbances broke out, effectively amounting to mutiny. Captain Lord Hervey's ship, the *Raissonable*, was one of many affected and, after being tried by court-martial, four ringleaders were condemned to death, three being executed on the 11th August and a fourth being reprieved at the very last moment before the sentence was carried out. The young seamen of the 1780s were really two generations removed from those Duncan had first sailed with as a captain's servant in 1746. Amongst this new breed, there seemed to be forces at work which had been absent in earlier times. Society was changing, men were becoming restless and were less willing to accept a naval regime which had remained unaltered for more than a century.

Figures released by the Admiralty in 1780 confirmed that, in the six years between 1774 and 1780, 175,990 men had enlisted. Of these, 1,243 had been killed, 18,541 had died from disease or accident and 42,069 had deserted. The extent to which there was discontent amongst the seamen was obvious for any intelligent person to discern.

In his new post in HMS *Edgar*, much of Captain Duncan's time was devoted to instructing young officers and this gave him the opportunity to organise his own thoughts on naval tactics, a topic of importance if he was ever to reach flag rank. The navy's fighting instructions were the subject of on-going debates. Whilst it was generally agreed the instructions should be tactically sound and properly understood by all officers, there were two schools of thought. One believed the emphasis should be on individual ship's captains taking the initiative in a naval action and, whilst conforming to the admiral's general plan as it had been explained beforehand, they should be able to sieze opportunities as they arose, be impetuous if necessary and take risks to break the enemy's line and achieve victory. The second school believed that, in a naval action, the fleet should act as a unit, forming line of battle, with each ship engaging her opposite number in the enemy's battle line, all ships aiming to break the enemy's main fleet.

The pendulum had swung between these two approaches over the years. In 1636, the policy had been to break the enemy's main fleet. Individual enemy ships which became disabled were disregarded and attention was concentrated on those which still had a fighting capability. Again, in 1654, the emphasis was on disabling the body of the enemy's fleet. No captain was permitted to leave the scene of battle and follow a lone enemy vessel. However, over the decades, this policy tended to encourage defensive thinking, so that some captains became loathe in battle ever to move away from the security of the fleet. This was the mentality which Captain Duncan knew had existed at the beginning of the first war in which he had served, namely the one which had ended in 1748.

However, later in that war, the policy had swung the other way and if an enemy ship was forced out of her line of battle, instructions required she should be pursued until taken or destroyed. This approach was also adopted during the Seven Years' War which ended in 1763. During the more recent war, and under the influence of Admiral Howe, fighting instructions had favoured the centralised approach. In 1777, Howe instructed that captains who forced enemy ships out of their line were to leave them and proceed to assist any British ship which was hard pressed. By 1782, he amended these instructions, reverting back to the wording originally used, namely: "None of His Majesty's Fleet shall pursue any small number of ships of the enemy until the main body of the enemy's fleet shall be disabled or shall run".

Howe's policy was to form line of battle, each ship then cutting behind the stern of her opposite number in the enemy's battle line, engaging her from leeward, firing at her hull and cutting off her retreat. The aim was to employ a rapid rate of fire at close range hoping the damage caused would force the enemy to surrender. The French, on the other hand, preferred to aim at longer range for masts and rigging, hoping this would immobilise the enemy ship at a distance and avoid action at close quarters.

There is no doubt that, from historical evidence, Duncan and his students could be proud of the qualities exhibited by many of Britain's naval commanders. They had often taken risks, or taken advantage of gaps developing in an enemy's line of battle, or exploited his mistakes. Many commanders had shown a high level of professionalism, efficiency and zest for action. But an important factor in battle had often been the sheer quality of seamanship exhibited, such as when it had been necessary to do battle in shallow, uncharted waters. British victories had not usually been achieved because of superior numbers. In fact, British ships tended to be smaller and less heavily armed than French or Spanish ones. Victories were achieved through squadrons manoeuvring more rapidly as a result of the better discipline, efficiency and cohesiveness of the British crews.

The high standard of gunnery in the Royal Navy had always been a vital factor, the best of British gun crews firing three shots to every two of the enemy's. The recently introduced carronade had taken a fearful toll of the enemy due to its high rate of fire and the ease with which it could be manouevred. Constant training of crews in seamanship, gunnery, close range fighting and grappling were absolutely essential. But the highest standards could only be achieved with good logistical backing and dockyard support for the maintenance of the ships. These were the messages that had to be transmitted to the young officers in the *Edgar* during Duncan's time in command.

The interpretation of fighting instructions, and the tactics used in a sea battle, were to be of considerable importance to Adam Duncan before the end of his career.

During his term of duty in command of the *Edgar*, Captain Duncan was called upon by the Civil Authority in Portsmouth to assist in quelling a riot. Sword in hand, and at the head of his party of armed sailors, he not only convinced the crowd that he had every intention of being obeyed but he did so by "joking them into good humour" and the riot broke up peacefully. (Reported in *The Times*, 19th October 1797).

His three year term of duty in HMS *Edgar* ended in 1786 and he was again placed on the Unemployed List on half pay. By the time he and Mrs Duncan left their home in Gosport to travel North to Scotland, they had seven children, Robert and Henry having been born during the captain's period in command of the *Edgar*.

Chapter 10 • THE CHANGING WORLD

MAJOR ALEXANDER DUNCAN NOW RESIDED in Lundie Castle with his wife, formerly Miss Smythe of Methven. Consequently, following their return to Scotland from Portsmouth in 1786, the captain's family spent much time at the home of Mrs. Duncan's parents, the Rt. Hon. and Mrs. Robert Dundas, in George Square, Edinburgh. The city had improved greatly since the early years of the century when the habits of the population and the sanitary arrangements left much to be desired. Sewage was no longer thrown each morning from the windows of the high tenements in the Old Town, although human excrement could still lie about in the closes leading to the flats for several days before it was cleared. Following the building of the New Town where Mr. and Mrs Dundas lived, classical squares, long straight streets and splendid houses with spacious gardens were appearing and this part of the city was clean and tidy.

Admiral Viscount Keppel, the man who had done most to further Duncan's career, died on the 2nd October 1786. The next year brought happier news, when the Admiralty informed Captain Duncan of his promotion to Rear-Admiral of the Blue to take effect from the 27th September 1787 but no offer of a peace-time command was forthcoming.

Rear-Admiral and Mrs. Duncan's family was finally completed by the birth of Catherine in 1788 and of Mary in 1790, the latter named after the wife of Sir William Duncan, Rear-Admiral Duncan's uncle. However, their second son, William, died in 1790 at the age of nine. Eventually, a tutor was required for the children and the admiral obtained the services of Robert Hood, a young man who was keen to become a minister of the church and who was studying hard to that end. The Duncan family became very fond of Mr. Hood and, when he eventually retired due to ill health, the admiral presented him with a silver garter and shoe buckles, the family giving him a Bible and a silver pencil-case. Robert Hood was an uncle of the poet Thomas Hood, who lived in the first half of the nineteenth century.

As a husband and father, Adam Duncan was exceedingly good natured, amiable, cheerful and kind. He was devoted to his wife and considered her to be the best woman in the world. He was careful with money and had a tendency at that time to feel financially insecure. At home, the Bible was read regularly to the children, family prayers were said before each meal and church was attended at least once on Sundays. However, his undoubted piousness never detracted from his lively and jovial nature.

Duncan's father-in-law, The Rt. Hon. Robert Dundas, Lord Advocate of Scotland, was elected the member of parliament for Edinburgh in 1790. He was a government minister with wideranging powers of patronage. Those, like the Duncans, living with such a political man, could not avoid being well-versed in the important issues of the day, such as the fight for independence in the North American colonies, the revolution in France, the publication of the book on the "Rights of Man" by Tom Paine, the activities of the Scottish Conventions and the Friends of the People movements.

The year 1789 had brought news of the mishandling by the British government of affairs in North America. The highly independent attitude of the thirteen colonies, and their resentment at interference from London, resulted in what had started as colonial insurgency ending with the inauguration of a new nation, the United States of America.

The revolution in France in 1789, which resulted in her king being beheaded and the "Directory" taking over the reins of government, strengthened the belief that the lower classes were no longer content to be treated as inferior beings, reacting without question to the whims of authority, be it in the form of a tyrannical landowner or a petty officer with a rope's end.

Of considerable interest to Robert Dundas, as a law officer of the Crown, and certainly a subject for discussion at his table, was Tom Paine's book, "The Rights of Man", published in 1791, and remarkable for selling 200,000 copies in a country which was still only semi-literate. It called for universal suffrage, the redistribution of property and for the abolition of titles, at the same time making a scathing attack on the British establishment. The book was considered a dangerous incitement to unrest and, in May 1792, it was banned by the government. This had the effect of dramatically increasing sales.

No one living in Edinburgh at this time could fail to be unaware of the Scottish Conventions movement which was working for electoral change and for an end to patronage. Between 1792 and 1794, there was support for this movement even amongst lawyers, academics and middle class tradesmen in Scotland. Also active in Edinburgh was a movement entitled "The Friends of the People", which attracted the support of men as prominent as Lieutenant-Colonel Dalrymple of Fordell.

But the movements demanding a greater democratisation of the country were not confined to literate men who wrote fine words. In Scotland in 1792, there were riots in Aberdeen, Perth, Dundee, Peebles, Lanark and Edinburgh where those involved demanded reform of the electoral process and expressed opposition to the established government and to its legal administrators. In Edinburgh, the riot was directed at the house of the Rt. Hon. Robert Dundas who, as the city's member of parliament, attracted the wrath of the rioters. About 1,400,000 people lived in Scotland at that time but, under the prevailing electoral law, only 4,000 of them were eligible to vote for the 45 members of parliament. This was the essence of the rioters' complaint.

The disturbance in Edinburgh took place on the king's birthday, the 4th June. Admiral Duncan was in the house in George Square with his mother-in-law, Mrs. Dundas, at the time the angry mob flung bricks and other objects through the windows. He went outside to calm the situation and, in the course of a scuffle, he received a blow from a stick. For the remainder of his life he needed to wear a double ring to support a finger which had been broken. Eventually, soldiers were called out, shots were fired and the mob dispersed.

On the 3rd February 1793, Rear-Admiral Duncan was promoted to the rank of Vice-Admiral and, later the same year, Great Britain found herself at war with France, the French Republican Army having invaded Holland. Yet again, despite his promotion, he received no offer of a command. He waited patiently, regularly visiting the Admiralty in London in the hope of being given an appointment. He knew the Royal Navy was fully stretched. Many French privateers were operating in the English Channel, the Bay of Biscay, the North Sea, the Baltic and in the Mediterranean whilst others operated further afield, attacking British shipping in the West Indies and East Indies from bases in Martinique, Guadalope and Mauritius. The navy had commitments which demanded that it maintain surveillance on a world-wide scale. It was found necessary for parliament to pass the Convoy Act, in 1793, requiring merchantmen to collect in various ports and form convoys before departing for distant shores. As many as five hundred merchantmen assembled regularly at Portsmouth, waiting for ships of the line and frigates to escort them through the known danger zones where the privateers operated.

During one of his regular visits to London, Duncan heard about the navy's great shortage of volunteers and how this had produced the hottest press ever to be implemented. The London River Press procured the bulk of its men from incoming merchantmen and colliers but numerous other press gangs were operating in coastal areas throughout the country. Some south coast towns were almost devoid of men, so many having fled into the countryside to avoid being pressed.

Those taken were assembled at the "rondy", as the headquarters of the press was called, before being put on board a reception tender. They were locked in the hold and guards with loaded muskets and fixed bayonets were mounted on deck. Usually, it took a day and a night in such conditions, often rat-infested, before the men were allocated to their ships. It was a thoroughly unpleasant experience and a poor introduction to the Royal Navy. The majority of the men were experienced seamen who worked efficiently after settling down in the service. In battle, they invariably performed well, always hopeful of becoming eligible for prize money.

The pressed men of this day were more fortunate than their predecessors. On entering the service they were medically examined and re-clothed, the latter greatly helping to reduce the incidence of typhus. At this time, the charge of fifteen shillings formerly made for treating a man with venereal disease was waived in the hope it would prevent men from concealing their condition.

By 1795 there was still a serious shortage of men for the navy and the Quota Acts were passed by parliament. These required each county, city and town to provide the navy with a stated number of men. A total of 9,764 were obtained in this way but many were the least desirable members of the community, being criminals or men awaiting trial.

1794 brought the news of Earl Spencer's appointment as First Lord of the Admiralty, a man with whom Duncan was to have much contact in the years ahead. Mr William Dundas, Mrs. Duncan's uncle, was Treasurer to the Navy and Secretary of State for War. Before his brother, Robert, was elected in 1790, William had been the member of parliament for Edinburgh.

In 1795, Holland signed an agreement promising to provide twelve sails of the line and eighteen frigates in support of the French. As the scope of the war widened, Vice-Admiral Duncan was appointed Commander-in-Chief of the North Sea Fleet in February 1795 and later, in June, was promoted to the rank of Admiral at the age of sixty-four.

Chapter 11 • THE MUTINOUS ROAD TO CAMPERDOWN

AS COMMANDER-IN-CHIEF OF THE NORTH SEA FLEET, Admiral Duncan, his hair now snowy white, was responsible for keeping the waters off the eastern coast of Britain between Harwich and the Shetland Islands under surveillance and free from the enemy. In particular, his tasks included blockading the entry to the Texel where the Dutch Fleet was anchored and ensuring that no invasion force destined for Britain sailed from there. But he was also required to take every opportunity to engage and destroy the Dutch Battle Fleet should it emerge from the Texel. He had under his command the *Glatton*, the *Lion*, the *Nassau* and the *Montagu* being four sails of the line in rather poor condition, together with the *Circe* frigate, two cutters and four luggers.

The navy's best ships had been despatched to the Mediterranean or were with the Channel squadrons and, to add to Duncan's difficulties, there was a constant transfer of vessels to and from his fleet. He was offered command in the Mediterranean in the summer of 1795 but he rejected it preferring, for reasons of health, to remain in a colder, northern climate. The North Sea Fleet was based at the Downs until May of 1796, when it moved to Yarmouth in Norfolk.

Initially, Admiral Duncan hoisted his flag on the *Prince George* but later, on the 31st March 1795, he transferred it to the *Venerable*, a seventy-four gun sail of the line, with William Hope in command as Flag Captain. The admiral now enjoyed a day cabin, where he could relax or hold briefing meetings with his subordinates; a large dining cabin, where he could enjoy his meals with the officers of the *Venerable* and his guests; and a sleeping cabin containing his cot with his washing and toilet cabinet, all cabins being sited in the stern of the ship. The *Venerable* was not in particularly good condition and, at times, rainwater dripped into some part of his accommodation. When the ship was in action, the admiral's quarters became an extension of one of the gun decks, all of his furniture having to be carefully stored so that guns could be moved into their firing positions.

This was Duncan's first command at flag rank but he adapted easily to his new station in life. He was now a mature and experienced officer in his sixty-fourth year. He had a thorough grasp of the duties of every grade of naval officer. He had served in each rank at sea under war conditions, except that of midshipman. He tried to get to know each officer, warrant officer and petty officer on his flagship by name and he took a deep and genuine interest in the people (the men of the lower deck). He always referred to them as "my lads" and it was invariably how he addressed them. With his gentlemanly erect bearing, pleasant demeanour and good manners he had developed about him a charisma to which all ranks responded. Many of his "lads" looked upon him as a grandfather figure. It was an age when men respected their elders and, to the younger sailors, he seemed to be very old and, therefore, deserving of much respect.

He was a natural leader, almost invariably cool and unflappable but, just occasionally, capable of losing his temper if his wishes were obstructed. His relaxed manner and the very size of the man seemed to give others confidence that what he said and did in any situation was correct. Whilst he was kind and humane, he always took for granted that others would perform their allotted duties with diligence and would behave in a disciplined manner. Unfortunately, with the constant changes in the ships under his command, he was not able to visit most crews frequently enough for them to get to know him well.

Shortly after assuming command in the North Sea, Duncan wrote to the Admiralty on several occasions, setting out his recommendations for improvements to the conditions under which men of the lower deck served. This was done because he sincerely believed they deserved to be treated and looked after better and, from his knowledge of life in the world beyond the navy, he also realised that many working men were now striving to achieve a better and fairer deal for themselves in the community. If they became frustrated, he knew from experience that riots and disturbances could be the result. He had a double ring on one hand to prove it.

Specifically, he asked for improvements to the men's diet including the provision of fresh fish, fresh food, lemon juice and sugar to guard against scurvy. He wanted wine for those who became sick and the regular provision of tobacco and soap. But he also recommended other changes including ensuring men were paid better and more regularly. He advised that leave should be granted as an entitlement rather than at the whim of ships' captains. He wanted dirty and unpleasant tasks to be shared equally amongst the crew rather than always being undertaken by the same men. He felt more petty officers should be appointed and that there should be a limit on the number of lashes which could be imposed by a court-martial. He wanted midshipmen to have no right to interfere with the crew and for young persons under the age of fifteen years to have a restricted alcohol quota. He believed that ships' chaplains should act as schoolmasters and that there should be a more equitable distribution of prize money. He wished to see the pressing of men into the service discontinued unless absolutely necessary. Duncan received no immediate response to his recommendations but maybe it was expecting too much of an overworked Admiralty, endeavouring at that time to direct naval warfare on a global scale.

In June 1795, Britain's ally, Russia, sent a squadron of twelve sails of the line and six frigates to augment Admiral Duncan's North Sea Fleet and to come under his command. He sailed to Texel with this enlarged fleet in August and again in November, hoping on the latter occasion, but without success, to intercept a convoy of Dutch merchantmen returning from the East Indies. When Duncan and the *Venerable* were not in the North Sea blockading the Texel, a continuous watch was maintained by a force positioned to form an inner ring of cutters sited close in-shore at the mouth of the Texel, with beyond, a middle ring composed of frigates and, finally, further out still in deeper water, at least two sails of the line. The ships on duty rotated, all regularly returning to the Downs or Yarmouth to replenish supplies.

About seven Dutch sails of the line and six frigates were known to be lying at anchor in the Texel. The observation and assessment of wind conditions were important factors for the blockade. It was unlikely the Dutch Fleet would come out of the Texel with a wind blowing from the West. On the other hand, it might easily emerge on an easterly wind and, under these conditions, the blockading force needed to comprise as many ships of the line as Admiral Duncan could muster. With a change in the wind from westerly to easterly, ships at Yarmouth would hurriedly weigh anchor and depart to join the blockade. In the absence of any other form of communication, cutters and luggers scurried to and fro across the North Sea carrying messages and orders.

In 1796, Major Alexander Duncan died and, having no children, the family estate at Lundie passed to Admiral Duncan. This made a great difference to his finances but it never altered his frugal life-style on board ship. In any event, he was in the middle of fighting a war and it never occurred to him to do other than continue to live and work as before.

Duncan and the *Venerable* lay off the Texel from March to May of 1796 before returning to Yarmouth. In the meantime, the British Cabinet had decided to take some positive offensive action against the Dutch by occupying the Helder Shore and Texel Island and, at the same time, by despatching fireships into the Texel to destroy the Dutch Fleet. The scheme did not meet with Duncan's approval because of the uncertainties of the weather in the North sea during the winter months and he also foresaw some danger should a westerly wind force his naval ships to retire well off-shore. This would leave the invading troops isolated in enemy territory for an uncertain length of time. The preparations of the expeditionary force took longer than expected and it was well into October before it left home shores. Continuous and persistently westerly winds made troop landings impossible and at the end of November the operation was aborted.

Towards the end of 1796, Vice-Admiral Richard Onslow was appointed Admiral Duncan's second-in-command and he hoisted his flag on the *Nassau*. There was a steady build-up in the number of ships in the North Sea Fleet. News from the Continent was of Dutch and French troops massing around the Texel and Dunkirk preparatory to invading Britain. Consequently, the *Venerable*, the *Albion*, the *Montagu* and the *Repulse*, later joined by the Russian Squadron, spent two months at sea blockading the Texel, breaking off when the wind turned westerly and arriving back in Yarmouth on the 23rd April 1797.

On the 18th April, during the absence of the *Venerable* and other ships of the North Sea Fleet, a petition had been presented to the Lords Commissioners of the Admiralty by a committee of seamen from the ships at Spithead, calling themselves "delegates of the fleet", elected to represent their fellows. The petition referred to the hardships and oppressions under which the seamen of His Majesty's navy had laboured for many years. Amongst other matters, it requested an increase in wages so that seamen might properly support their wives and families, the provision of vegetables and better quality food weighed out in the same way as it is in the commercial trade of the country, better provision for the sick on board ship, better arrangements for shore leave and, finally, for men who were wounded, to continue to be paid until well again and discharged.

The document was well-prepared and respectful, the delegates making reasonable requests for an improvement to their conditions of service. All grades of men appeared to be involved in the "dispute" including both sailors and marines. During discussions which followed the presentation of the petition, complaints were made about individual officers who were regarded as behaving tyrannically. Essentially, the petition dealt with those matters on which Admiral Duncan had made recommendations to the Admiralty from as far back as 1795. By the time the *Venerable* returned to Yarmouth on the 23rd April the Admiralty had agreed to some of the delegates' requests. Also, King George had signed a pardon in order to ensure they would not be victimised for their action. However, parliament had to approve the money needed to finance the changes and, unfortunately, there was some delay in this during which complications developed in the ships located away from Spithead.

Vice-Admiral Onslow repaired on board the *Venerable* as soon as she anchored in Yarmouth on the 23rd April and briefed Admiral Duncan on the events which had taken place at Spithead during his absence. As the delegates' requests had been met and as the king had signed a pardon, both felt matters should rapidly return to normal. The admiral's views appeared to be confirmed by a letter he received from the men of the *Venerable* on the 27th April, expressing their thanks to the Admiralty for agreeing to the requests of the Spithead men and giving assurance of their loyalty to their "worthy commander-in-chief".

Admiral Duncan was in his day cabin on the afternoon of the 30th April when he heard a noisy disturbance and rowdy cheering emanating from the for'ard part of the ship. He knew at once that the men must have abandoned their duties. He sent his orderly with messages to Captain Hope and to the captain of marines in which he ordered the former to muster all officers and the latter to muster his marines under arms. Giving some minutes for his orders to be implemented, he made his way to the quarterdeck where the officers and armed marines were already assembled whilst the crew were crowded together on the forecastle. There was a hubbub of noise and the admiral stood silent for a moment, his face red, his hands tightening as he endeavoured to control his anger. In a loud and authoritative voice, he demanded to be told the reason for such improper conduct. There was a deathly silence. He reminded his lads that their country was at war and facing imminent invasion. He reminded them they had just had the promise of improved pay and conditions and then he repeated his question, "What is the reason for this indiscipline and improper conduct?" Receiving no reply, he selected five of the crew whom he knew to be capable of expressing themselves coherently, ordered them aft to the poop and, in stentorian voice instructed the remainder of the crew to go below.

Discussion with the chosen five elucidated rather vague reasons for the crew's behaviour. The men believed they were doing no more than those at Spithead had done. They didn't see any harm in it. The admiral pointed out how their conduct was close to mutiny and he invited them to tell him what matters were causing concern. Effectively, they wanted to know when they would get their increased pay and better provisions. The admiral assured them he was doing everything possible to speed up both matters.

After dismissing the five, Duncan ordered all hands to muster on the quarterdeck where, in a calm, more fatherly voice, he explained how the Spithead men's requests already approved by the Admiralty would be put into effect throughout the whole of the fleet as soon as possible. He reminded the crew that acts of indiscipline were regarded very seriously and he made it clear there was no circumstance in which he would have his orders disobeyed or his flag disgraced. A few days later, he received a letter from the men which repeated how they had merely wanted to support their fellow seamen at Spithead and how they had not intended this to be taken as rebellious or mutinous. They confirmed their loyalty to their admiral and to the officers.

Duncan did not respond until the 7th May when he called the crew together and addressed them. To aid his memory, he referred frequently to a number of old envelopes on the back of which he had written some notes. He berated the men for setting a bad example to the other ships in his fleet and he went on to say, "You see me now, grown grey with fifty-one years' service. In every ship I had the honour to command, I have endeavoured to do justice both to the public and the men I commanded, and have often been flattered with particular marks of their regard. I still hope, in spite of all that has happened, this ship's company has not lost their confidence in me. Both my officers and I are always ready to redress any supposed grievances when asked in a proper manner." He scolded the sailors for the bad language he frequently heard them using and advised them to pay more respect to God. He ended, "God bless you all and may He always have us under His gracious protection and make us better men." Afterwards, he received a letter from the crew assuring him of their loyalty and, in subsequent weeks and months, that loyalty never faltered.

However, incidents similar to that which occurred on the *Venerable* were reported by the captains of almost all the ships at Yarmouth. In each case, Admiral Duncan repaired on board the offending vessel, had his flag hoisted and the crew assembled. His initial remarks left no doubt in the men's minds that rebellious conduct would not be tolerated in any ship in his fleet. He always went on to find out what grievances his men were harbouring and he promised to see that the changes approved by the Admiralty were rapidly implemented. His voice was strong when he spoke but there was no aggression in it. He chose his words carefully, for he knew he was walking a tightrope.

From his experience over many years, he knew sailors wanted to be treated as human beings and to be able to voice their grievances from time to time. They needed someone in authority to listen although they never expected to get everything they asked for. Duncan knew he could do no more than contain the problem since external forces were influencing the men. There was no possibility of extinguishing the flames. Too many men had been treated too badly for too long.

Duncan was constantly in touch with Earl Spencer, the First Lord of the Admiralty, reporting to him on events within his own fleet and receiving from his lordship regular news of the situation elsewhere. On the 12th May, he was told the mutiny had spread to ships at the Nore. The *Sandwich* was the first ship to be affected and others followed. Officers were ordered ashore and a man called Richard Parker was appointed "president" by the men's committee of delegates. The several demands made earlier by the men at Spithead which had not been met in the Admiralty's response, were being given as the reasons for the rebelliousness at the Nore. These related to leave entitlement, the distribution of prize money and the easing of the punishment code.

This news brought no joy to Duncan's heart since the Nore was close enough to Yarmouth for there to be collusion between the two bases. However, troubles arose closer to home during the next day, the 13th May, when there was a serious disturbance on the *Adamant*. The admiral repaired on board immediately. He asked if any man disputed his authority or that of his officers. One of the crew stepped forward. Duncan's response was immediate. The onlookers were held spell-bound

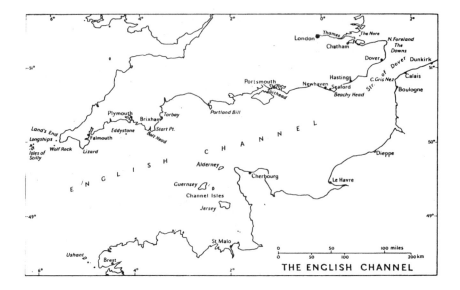

THE ENGLISH CHANNEL

as he grasped the man by the collar, jerked him over the side of the ship and left him dangling there. Turning to face the crew, Duncan announced, "My lads! Look at this fellow who dares to deprive me of the command of the fleet!"

There were roars of laughter. The news spread round the ships at Yarmouth and never again did any man dare to question their admiral's authority. Thereafter, in the difficult days ahead, the crew of the *Adamant* remained faithful to him.

The trouble at Spithead was over by the 17th May and the fleet there had weighed anchor and departed for the English Channel under the command of Admiral Lord Bridport but a difficult situation now arose in respect of the Nore mutineers. Admiral Duncan's views were asked on the possibility of his ships at Yarmouth being used to subdue the mutinous ships. He thought long and hard about the proposal. He had heard rumours suggesting the Nore men were planning to sail their ships into enemy ports or even to America. Could he stand by and watch this happen? If he ordered the loyal crews of his fleet to fire upon their compatriots in the Nore ships, would they obey? Might the proposal not succeed in making matters worse rather than better? He replied to the Admiralty that, whereas he would not shrink from undertaking the task of dealing with the Nore men if this was considered to be the only way forward, he felt it would be creating much bad feeling between his men and others in the service and was better avoided.

The activities of the Dutch Fleet now interceded, for it became known that eighteen sails of the line, twenty-two frigates with sloops and brigs, together with forty-two large troop transports were lying in the Texel awaiting a favourable easterly wind before embarking on their long-expected invasion of Britain. However the wind remained in the West for several days during which a deputation from the Nore attempted to make contact with the Yarmouth crews. Realising the vulnerability of his men to further incitement to mutiny, Duncan decided his ships must leave Yarmouth the next day, whatever the wind direction.

On the evening of the 26th May Duncan held a conference in the *Venerable* to assess the likely reaction of the various ship's crews if he ordered the fleet to set sail the next morning. The *Nassau* men were refusing to sail until their wages were paid. The captains of the other ships believed their people would obey orders but, despite this, Duncan felt uneasy. It was decided Vice-Admiral Onslow would transfer his flag from the *Nassau* to the *Adamant*.

The noise of cordage moving and blocks jangling was resounding through the ships by five o'clock the next morning as the North Sea Fleet prepared to put to sea. With the *Venerable* was the *Adamant*, the *Agamemnon*, the *Belliqueux*, the *Lion*, the *Glatton*, the *Standard*, the *Leopard*, the *Monmouth*, the *Ardent*, the *Isis* and the *Repulse*, with the smaller ships the *Garland* frigate, the *Stork* sloop, the *Trent* and the *Circe*. Around noon, when all vessels were under sail, the *Belliqueux* passed under the stern of the *Venerable*. Duncan had a signal sent ordering her to come to the wind on the larboard tack like the *Venerable*. The *Belliqueux* responded by hoisting a flag, half white and red over half blue and yellow, being the signal of inability. With the *Standard*, she deserted the fleet and returned to Yarmouth to wait there until the men were paid.

By one hour after noon on the 29th, the *Venerable* and the *Adamant* were under sail for the Texel with the *Circe*, a twenty-eight gun frigate, the *Garland* and the small vessels the *Trent* and the *Stork*, the remaining ships having deserted their admiral at the moment he was sailing to face the enemy. It was beyond Duncan's comprehension that men could act in this way. Clearly, times had changed since his early days with Commander Haldane in West Highland waters and with Commodore Keppel at Havana. Men behaved differently in this modern age, as he knew all too well from the years recently spent in Edinburgh. One could hardly blame him for feeling isolated and despondent. However, resilient characters do not remain despondent for long. His North Sea Fleet, albeit greatly diminished in numbers, had a job to do and, if it was God's will, it would be done.

Chapter 12 • DUNCAN'S PHANTOM FLEET

ALTHOUGH NOW IN HIS SIXTY-SIXTH YEAR, Admiral Duncan was fitter than many men half his age. He was slower than in his younger days but he attributed that, not to age, but to the inevitable increase in weight which had come with the advance of years. When the *Venerable* came in sight of the Texel on the evening of the 30th May, he felt it essential that he should himself observe the nature and strength of the enemy. He walked along the gangway joining the quarterdeck to the forecastle, stopping to converse briefly with one of his "lads". Reaching the forecastle, he swung his body out over the waist of the ship, put his foot on the lowest ratline and grasped the shrouds with his hands. On his way up, he spurned the lubber's hole and with his body in a semi-horizontal position and looking skywards, he negotiated the futtock shrouds, arriving shortly afterwards at the top.

He looked into the Texel, then put his glass to his eye and scanned the river channel to the East. In view were fourteen sail of the line, eight frigates and about one hundred transports and supply ships. He could counter this armada with his flagship of seventy-four guns, the *Adamant* of fifty guns and a few small vessels.

Vice-Admiral Onslow, and Captain Hotham who commanded the *Adamant*, were rowed over to the *Venerable* late that evening and they met Admiral Duncan in his day cabin as the light faded. Onslow was quick to point out that the *Venerable* and the *Adamant* could be attacked, not merely by the Dutch squadrons advancing out of the Texel but, if matters went badly wrong in England, by the mutinous ships from the Nore. As there was no possibility their two ships could survive an attack from either superior force, Onslow suggested they should retreat to Leith Roads in the River Forth in Scotland at the first sign of trouble. Duncan would have none of this, claiming laughingly he would be accused of wanting to see his wife and family if he set foot in Scotland, since Mrs. Duncan was at home in Lundie with the children at this time.

Duncan outlined his plan of action. The channel of the Texel was so narrow that only one vessel at a time could negotiate it. The *Venerable* and the *Adamant* would anchor in the channel one astern of the other

---

DUNCAN OF CAMPERDOWN

and, if attacked, they would both fight until they were sunk. Soundings would be taken to locate an anchorage for the *Venerable* where, if she went down, his admiral's flag would always fly above the surface of the water.

But another scheme was hatched. The sails of the line would be constantly active in flag-signalling to the ships of a phantom fleet lying just beyond the horizon and ostensibly out of view of ships anchored in the Texel. Duncan's small ships would appear to be active, repeatedly sailing westwards to the horizon with imaginery messages from the flagship and being seen repeatedly returning eastwards for fresh instructions. But the small vessels had another task. They had to ensure no Dutch fishing vessels or other small craft passed in or out of the Texel since the cover for the whole operation could be blown. If the Dutch Admiral John William de Winter, flying his flag on the *Vrijheid*, got wind of the deception, the *Venerable* and the *Adamant*, together with their crews, would stand little chance of surviving. One thing was certain, Admiral Duncan would never surrender. It would be a fight to the death.

As always, Duncan wanted to keep his lads informed of his plans, so all officers and men in the *Venerable* were mustered early on the morning of the 1st June. He told them how sad he was that his fleet had deserted him and most glowingly thanked the officers, seamen and marines of the *Venerable* for their support. He reminded them how, often in the past, they had looked into the Texel and seen enemy ships which were fearful of meeting them. He explained his plan of action and promised that if they survived, they would return to the Nore and deal with the misguided men who had deserted. He asked for God's blessing on them all and, by the time he had finished, there were lumps in many throats.

At this particular moment, Great Britain was at her most vulnerable. Whilst the Channel Fleet was blockading the French ports from which an invasion could be launched, the Texel was being blockaded only by two sails of the line and a phantom squadron. The time was never more ripe for an invasion of Britain from the Texel, particularly if the French army units at Brest moved rapidly into Holland and combined with the invasion force already there. Only Duncan and his squadron stood in their way. However, whilst the crews of Duncan's two sails of the line remained loyal and devoted to him and to their task, Captain Halkett, commander of the *Circe*, together with Lieutenant Richardson had to remain on deck with loaded weapons night and day guarding against a possible insurrection by some of their crew who had already occupied the lower part of the ship, and were only waiting for an appropriate moment to take the *Circe* over and return to Yarmouth or the Nore.

For three days and three nights the wind blew from the East and the crews were at quarters for the entire period without sleep. A moment of relaxation in the scheme of subterfuge, or slackness in letting through a small boat acting as a spy for de Winter, could have spelt disaster.

On the 4th June, the wind came round to westward and, for the moment, the crisis had passed. The *Venerable* and the *Adamant* moved away, leaving the small vessels, the *Trent*, the *Stork* and the *Joke* lugger to continue observation on the enemy. Duncan's force was increased on this day with the arrival of the *Sanspareil* and the *Russell*, a seventy-four gun sail of the line. Further reinforcements arrived on the 9th June in the form of the *Prince*, the *Formidable*, the *Caesar*, the *Bedford*, the *Ganges* and the *Glatton*, joining the *Venerable* about ten miles South East of the Texel. Intelligence reports reaching Duncan indicated eighty thousand French troops were now based in Holland and ready to take part in the proposed invasion of Britain. With the arrival off Texel of the Russian Squadron under Rear-Admiral Makaroff, the North Sea Fleet was again up to fighting strength. However, Makaroff's squadron returned to Russia ten days later.

News of the final collapse of the mutiny at the Nore reached Admiral Duncan on the 17th June. Since discipline could be better maintained at sea, his intention now was to keep his fleet off Texel for as long as possible, and this he did for nineteen weeks revictualling from store-ships at sea. To Duncan's great satisfaction his ships received a continuous supply of wine, fresh meat and water, sent by the Admiralty.

In July, Vice-Admiral Onslow moved his flag to the *Monarch*. The *Ardent*, the *Director*, the *Belliqueux* and the *Isis* joined the North Sea Fleet indicating that the men, after all, had decided to support their admiral. Severe storms battered the ships for some days in August when a further two sails of the line, the *Monmouth* and the *Agincourt* augmented Duncan's fleet. On the 26th September, the Admiralty ordered the North Sea vessels to Yarmouth for provisioning and refitting since the latest intelligence reports gave grounds for believing the Dutch had postponed their invasion plans. Leaving small vessels to observe the Texel, Duncan's ships arrived off Yarmouth on the 1st October.

Early on the morning of the 9th October, the *Vestal* lugger arrived in Yarmouth with news that the Dutch Fleet had sailed out of the Texel.

Immediately, Admiral Duncan ordered eleven of his sails of the line to put to sea and he instructed the other ships to follow him as soon as possible. The Squadron departed from Yarmouth Roads at eleven o'clock in the morning and by two o'clock on the next afternoon, the 10th October, it was close to the Texel. At last, after two years, there might be an opportunity to bring the Dutch Fleet to battle.

Chapter 13 • THE BATTLE OF CAMPERDOWN:

"Up wi' the hel-lem and gang into the middle o'it!"

BY SIX O'CLOCK ON THE MORNING of the 11th October 1797, and after a good night's rest, Admiral Duncan was already on the quarterdeck. Beside him was Captain Fairfax, his Flag Captain. The sky was clear and there was a brisk wind from the Nor' Nor' West carrying the *Venerable* under full sail in the direction of the Dutch coast. Seven of his ships were manned by men who had been involved in the recent mutiny and had returned to support him. He was pleased they had relented and, understanding the hardships under which they had served in the past, he was willing to forgive them.

Since the enemy might be sighted at any time, Duncan mustered the crew. As he came before them on the quarterdeck they fell silent, the only noise being the flapping of canvas in the wind and the crashing of water against the hull. He said nothing for a few moments to allow each man to be with his own thoughts. Then he called them to prayer, committed them all to God and asked for His protection in the coming battle.

The departure of the North Sea Fleet from Yarmouth had been reported to Admiral de Winter by a fishing vessel and he was now intent upon reaching the safety of the Texel and avoiding battle. His ships were of shallow draft and they could sail much closer to the shore than could the British ships. At nine o'clock, Admiral Duncan received a message from the *Circe* informing him the Dutch fleet had been sighted about nine miles to the South East and five miles off-shore of the coastal villages of Egmont and Camperdown. At that location the Texel was about fifteen miles to the North East. The enemy force consisted of sixteen sails of the line, five frigates and five brigs. Admiral Duncan also had sixteen sails of the line under his command together with two frigates, a sloop, four cutters and a lugger.

On receipt of the message from the *Circe*, the admiral turned to Captain Fairfax, his Flag Captain, "Make a general signal," he said, "Prepare for Battle!"

Fairfax instructed his signal midshipman, John Neale, and within minutes the appropriate flags were darting up the halliards. From now on Duncan was constantly observing the position of each ship, endeavouring to ensure they kept together as they approached the scene of battle. At fifteen minutes past nine o'clock he saw the *Circe* lagging behind and ordered, "Signal to Circe. Come within hail!" followed immediately by, "Signal to Russell. Close with the Admiral!"

At this moment, one of the *Venerable*'s young officers approached Admiral Duncan and asked him how many Dutch ships they were about to engage. "Really, sir," Duncan replied, "I cannot be certain, but when we have taken them we will count them!"

Duncan had lectured to young officers on the subject of naval tactics and the fighting instructions when he had been captain of the *Edgar* at Portsmouth fourteen years earlier. Now all he had taught could be put into practice. His ships would form line of battle as, no doubt, would the enemy's. Each would then bear down upon the vessel in the corresponding position in the enemy line. In order that a start could be made to forming this line of battle, he ordered, "Make a general signal. Line on a starboard bearing!"

By ten o'clock, he formed the opinion his ships were not making enough speed and he ordered, "General signal. Make more sail!"

A little later, the *Isis* and the *Lancaster* did not appear to respond and the admiral ordered the signal to be repeated for their benefit. Through his glass, he could see the *Russell* veering too much to larboard and he ordered, "Signal to Russell. Steer more to starboard!"

The *Isis* fell behind again and her captain received the instruction "Make more sail!". Anticipating the moment of contact with the enemy, he ordered, "Make a general signal. To engage the enemy as you arrive up to them!" However, Captain Inglis, commanding the *Belliqueux* became rather confused with the proliferation of the admiral's signals. In a temper, he flung his signal book on the deck, and in his unmistakably Scottish voice, roared, "Damn! Up wi' the hel-lem and gang into the middle o'it!"

For the next hour, by a continuous flow of signals, the admiral directed operations as his fleet advanced towards the enemy. However,

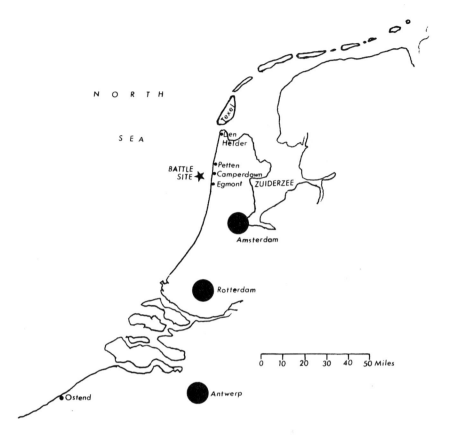

by thirty five minutes past eleven o'clock, he decided there was a grave danger the Dutch would escape. He could not risk sailing at the speed of his slowest ship merely to keep his vessels together so they could form a line of battle at the moment of contact with the enemy. Therefore, he ordered, "General signal. Bear up and sail large!" followed by, "General signal. To pass through the enemy's line and engage them to leeward!" These orders allowed each captain to go at his fastest speed and to engage the enemy at the earliest possible moment, aiming to get between the enemy and the shore to prevent his escape.

It was five minutes past noon when the admiral ordered, "Make a general signal. Close action!"

The North Sea Fleet was now moving towards the Dutch ships in two divisions, the most northerly led by Duncan himself in the *Venerable* with the *Bedford*, the *Ardent*, the *Triumph*, the *Belliqueux*, the *Lancaster*, the *Isis* and the *Circe* frigate whilst the more southerly division was led by Vice-Admiral Onslow in the *Monarch* with the *Russell*, the *Director*, the *Montagu*, the *Monmouth*, the *Powerful*, the *Veteran*, the *Adamant* and the *Agincourt*. The British approach to the attack was two pronged. On the other hand, the Dutch ships were formed up in classic line of battle orientated North East to South West. The *Vrijheid*, Admiral de Winter's flagship, was positioned in the northern section of the Dutch line of battle whilst Rear Admiral Reyntjes, in the *Jupiter*, was near the rear.

The guns of the *Jupiter* opened up at thirty minutes past noon as she fired a broadside at the *Monarch*, Vice-Admiral Onslow's flagship. This signalled the commencement of what has come to be known as the Battle of Camperdown. From the quarterdeck of the *Venerable*, Admiral Duncan could see that Onslow was holding his fire despite repeated broadsides from the *Jupiter*. He continued to do so until the *Monarch* was lying between the *Jupiter* and the *Haarlem*, the ship astern of her. Only then did her larboard and starboard guns simultaneously fire broadsides which ripped devastatingly through both her opponents.

Admiral de Winter's flagship, the *Vrijheid* was lying fifth from the van of the Dutch fleet and it was on her that Admiral Duncan bore down, with the *Bedford* and the *Ardent* in close support. He presented only his bow to the *Vrijheid* and refrained from using his bow chasers since these tended to reduce the ship's speed. Emitting one thunderous roar after another, the Dutch ships continuously fired broadsides at Duncan's approaching division. Not until he was close to the enemy did Duncan order "Helm hard a-starboard", bringing the *Venerable* into a position from which she could respond.

With an ear-splitting roar from her larboard guns, the *Venerable* fired her first broadside. Flames and smoke disgorged from her thirty-two pounders and swirled back into the lower gundeck through the open ports, engulfing the gun crews. The old ship jerked violently as her guns recoiled. They were sponged out and trundled forward again by pigtailed gunners, stripped to the waist, with neckerchiefs tied around their heads to protect their eardrums from the noise. Before they could fire again, the larboard twenty-four pounders on the middle gundeck added their contribution by emitting a deafening boom and despatching round shot towards the Dutch flagship in the hope of battering and splintering her hull. Over and over again the process was repeated, the gun teams able to fire another salvo every ninety seconds, sometimes round shot to cause structural damage,

British sails of the line

 British frigates

 Dutch sails of the Line

 Dutch frigates

 Dutch ship which struck her colours and surrendered

 Direction of movement

BRITISH

		GUNS
A	Venerable	74
B	Ardent	64
C	Triumph	74
D	Isis	50
E	Bedford	74
F	Lancaster	64
G	Belliqueux	64
H	Monarch	74
I	Powerful	74
J	Russel	74
K	Monmouth	64
L	Veteran	64
M	Agincourt	64
N	Adamant	50
O	Director	64
P	Montagu	74

FRIGATES

Q	Beaulieu	40
R	Circe	28
S	Martin	16

DUTCH

		GUNS
1	Vryheid	74
2	States General	74
3	Wassenaer	64
4	Cerberus	68
5	Beschermer	56
6	Leyden	68
7	Batavier	56
8	Jupiter	74
9	Haarlem	68
10	Alkmaar	56
11	Delft	56
12	Gelykheid	68
13	Mars	44
14	Admiral Devries	68
15	Brutus	74
16	Hercules	64

FRIGATES

17	Munnikendem	44
18	Ambuscade	32

Three more Frigates, names unknown, and five Brigs.

sometimes shot designed to tear rigging and, at other times, anti-personnel grape shot.

But the *Vrijheid* was not idle. Those on the *Venerable* saw the black muzzles of her guns viciously spit fire and smoke, followed seconds later by the whine of shot, some landing in the sea and sending up plumes of water, others whistling ominously overhead. The *Vrijheid*'s guns kept firing broadside after broadside. One shot struck a carronade on the *Venerable*'s upper deck, knocking it off its slide. Another damaged her rigging and carried away Admiral Duncan's flag. Six times his flag was shot to pieces and six times it was replaced. Through breaks in the smoke, shot could be seen ricocheting across the crests of the waves as, like bouncing torpedos, they sped in the *Venerable*'s direction. One struck and penetrated her hull with a thud, the sound of ripping timber mingling with the muffled cries from below-decks where men had been trapped under fallen debris. The noise was becoming more intense by the minute until it was nearly unbearable. The dense smoke in the gundecks made it difficult to breathe. On the quarterdeck, the signal midshipman, John Neale, ducked his head as he heard a shot come over. The admiral called to him, "Very well, my boy. That is all very well. But don't do it again. You might put your head in the way of the shot!"

Desperately, Duncan wanted to break the enemy line and stand on to the leeward (inshore) side of the *Vrijheid*. He saw his chance and ordered the helm hard a-larboard expecting to pass under the stern of the Dutch flagship. He was thwarted by the *States General* which moved forward into the line of battle, close to the *Vrijheid*'s stern blocking the *Venerable*'s intended move. With skilful seamanship, Duncan's order to run the *Venerable* under the stern of the *States General* instead was successfully carried out. In the process, the *Venerable*'s larboard carronades loaded with musket balls smashed the Dutchman's stern, dismounted some of her guns and killed many of her crew. The *States General* was forced out of the line although she still had the capability for some very aggressive gunnery. The *Venerable* had broken the enemy's line. Shortly after one o'clock in the afternoon nearly all the British ships were between the Dutch and the shore. One of Admiral Duncan's objectives had been achieved.

Noise, flames and smoke dominated the scene of the action. The *Ardent*, lying off the larboard side of the *Vrijheid*, was engaged in a ferocious battle with her during which the *Ardent*'s captain, Richard Burgess, was killed

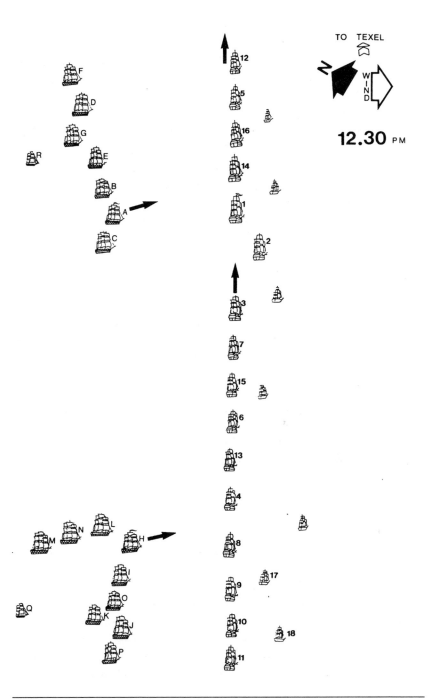

TO TEXEL

WIND

12.30 PM

along with thirty-nine others. A total of ninety-six men were wounded. The ship's surgeon, Richard Young, who had to work without any assistance, was so hard-pressed he was forced to carry out amputations without making the patients drunk beforehand, a procedure regarded as an essential in the days before anaesthetics.

The *Bedford* was engaged with the *De Vries* whilst the *Belliqueux*, the *Isis* and the *Lancaster* fought it out with the *Hercules*, the *Beschermer* and the *Gelijkheid*. Further South, Vice-Admiral Onslow had broken the enemy's line but of that, Duncan could see nothing since the *Venerable* was now under very concentrated attack from several quarters. On her larboard side, she was under fire from the *Vrijheid's* starboard guns and to starboard from the *States General's* larboard guns. She was also under fire from the stern guns of the *De Vries* and from broadsides fired from the larboard guns of the *Wassenaer* astern of her.

From forward to aft, every gun on the *Venerable* was continuously in action for another two hours. There was a constant movement of gun crews from the larboard to the starboard side of the ship in virtual darkness and in an atmosphere dense with pungent fumes. William Balchin, William Clark, Thomas Ellis and the other powder monkeys were on the point of total exhaustion through trying to keep pace with the rate at which the guns were being fired, as they raced from the magazine to the gun decks with the powder cartridges. Sometimes, the *Venerable* would fire on a down roll and the shots would smash through the enemy's hull. At other times, she would fire on an up roll and the enemy's rigging would fall victim to her projectiles. She had four opponents to contend with simultaneously and everyone was called upon to make a superhuman effort, be he volunteer or pressed man. Both British and Dutch ships were withstanding murderous broadsides at near point-blank range. This was proving one of the fiercest naval battles ever fought.

Periodically, the admiral felt the *Venerable* judder as yet another shot hit some part of her structure. Constantly, there was the hiss and whine of shot hurtling overhead, the thunder of the guns and the reverberations as they recoiled after firing. A shot shattered the maintopgallant mast and, for the seventh time, the *Venerable* was no longer flying its admiral's flag. Men, sails and splinters of mast collapsed on to the deck or fell overboard. Duncan saw his flag amongst the wreckage and went forward to retrieve it. Since part of the mast was missing, the flag could no longer be run

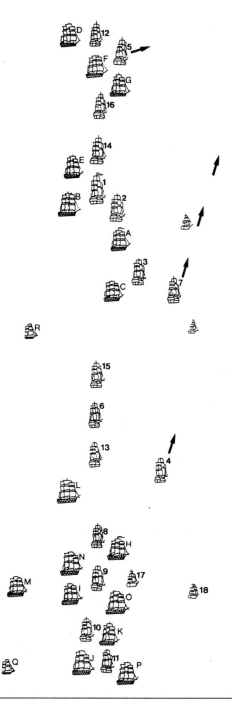

up in the usual manner. Duncan looked at it forlornly and then up at the broken mast as more shot continued to whine dangerously overhead.

Ordinary Seaman Jack Crawford, who had been fighting the after gun on the starboard side, stepped forward and offered to carry it aloft. "Go aloft, John," the admiral said. "Nail the colours up."

His words were lost in the noise of battle. Without hesitation, Jack clambered up the shrouds, marlinspike in hand. A shot struck the mast close to his face and thrust a splinter of wood through his cheek. Undaunted, he stood on the topmast cap, nailed the upper end of the flag as far up as he could reach and nailed its lower end down close to the cap. Then he slid down the topmast backstay and jumped on to the deck to cheers from his shipmates and an expression of concern from the admiral for his injury. "Never mind, sir," said Jack, "it's nothing".

Suddenly, through the smoke and fog of war, a ball of fire and intense light arose from the surface of the water high into the sky as if a volcano had erupted. Through the open gun ports, shafts of the light penetrated into the gundecks of the ships. For a time, men could actually see clearly the faces of their fellows. During the battle between the *Triumph* and the *De Vries*, a shot from one of the *Triumph*'s carronades had hit and ignited a powder cask on the *Hercules*, one of the Dutch sails of the line. Her sails, rigging and deck instantly became a ball of flame as she drifted out of control. It took many hours before the fire was extinguished.

It was now two o'clock in the afternoon. The sixty-four gun ship, the *Wassenaer*, had suffered enough from the guns of the *Venerable* and she struck her colours at about this time. The *Venerable*'s main mast, fore mast, mizen mast and bowsprit had been lost or damaged and she needed continual pumping to keep her afloat. Thirteen seamen and two marines had been killed and six officers, fifty-two seamen and four marines had been wounded. Injured men lay or sat dazed upon the decks whilst fragments of others dangled from the rigging. Sharp slivers of planking from the deck lay all around. The savage gunfire continued, now mainly coming from the *Vrijheid*, the *States General* having disappeared in a cloud of smoke as she scurried from the scene of battle towards the Texel.

As the hour of three o'clock approached, it was becoming increasingly difficult for their helmsmen to control the movements of both the *Vrijheid* and the *Venerable* on account of the damage they had sustained to their rigging and rudders. As a result, they drifted apart until the distance between them was about half a mile.

TO TEXEL

N

WIND

2.0 PM

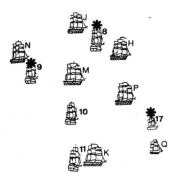

The pressure was taken off the *Venerable* with the arrival on the scene of the *Director* and the *Powerful* both from Vice Admiral Onslow's southern division. In the South, the *Haarlem*, the *Jupiter* and the *Monnikendem* had already struck their colours. But more assistance for the admiral's flagship came from the North, in the form of the *Lancaster* and the *Belliqueux*.

Through his glass, Admiral Duncan could see Captain Bligh, in the *Director*, continuing the assault on the *Vjirheid*, firing at point-blank range. Shortly after three o'clock, the Dutch flagship had lost all her masts and her guns were, one after the other, becoming silent. Suddenly, at fifteen minutes past three o'clock, an unnatural stillness fell upon the scene of battle. It was disturbed only by the sound of the wind in sails, by the lapping of water against hulls, and by the awful, agonising wails of the mangled and mortally wounded men awaiting surgical attention or death and hoping that one or the other would not be too long in coming.

His eye riveted to his glass, Duncan detected the *Circe* jolly-boat being rowed over to the Dutch flagship and, shortly afterwards, saw it approach with the lonely figure of Admiral de Winter, the Commander-in-Chief of the defeated Dutch Fleet, seated in the sternsheets. In due course, on the quarterdeck of the *Venerable*, de Winter proffered his sword to Admiral Duncan. Shaking his head and holding out his hand, Duncan said, "I would much rather take a brave man's hand than his sword."

Later, Admiral de Winter conceded he had lost the fight because Duncan, rather than waiting to form line of battle, had chosen to break the Dutch line as quickly as possible and move to its leeward side making escape impossible.

Shortly after receiving Admiral de Winter, Duncan mustered his crew and said prayers in thankfulness for their victory and for the protection which the Almighty had provided. He then despatched a letter to the Admiralty informing them of the victorious outcome of the battle. Eleven Dutch ships had been taken as prizes, including the *Vrijheid* (74 guns), the *De Vries* (68 guns), the *Gelijkheid* (68 guns), the *Wassenaer* (64 guns), the *Jupiter* (74 guns), the *Haarlem* (68 guns), the *Alkmaar* (56 guns), the *Delft* (56 guns), the *Hercules* (64 guns), the *Monnikendem* (44 guns) and the *Ambuscade* (32 guns). Seven sails of the line escaped into the Texel. Eleven ships taken out of the eighteen involved was a remarkable achievement. It was more than twice the number taken at the Battle of St. Vincent.

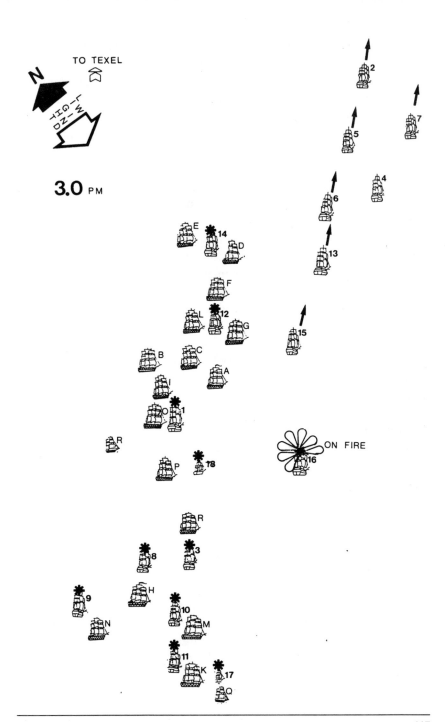

The tactics Admiral Duncan adopted when he decided not to form line of battle but, instead, to attack as two groups, one thrusting at the centre and one at the rear of the enemy's line, were those later employed by Vice-Admiral Lord Nelson at Trafalgar. In Nelson's case, the form of attack was decided upon beforehand; in Duncan's case, it represented a change of plan, adopted on the spur of the moment to prevent the enemy from escaping.

The *Venerable* arrived back in Yarmouth on the 18th October 1797. Admiral Duncan and his men were greeted enthusiastically. His victory had destroyed a significant part of the enemy's navy and, for the time being, had removed from Great Britain the threat of invasion by troops based in Holland. He was created Viscount Duncan of Camperdown and Baron Duncan of Lundie, awarded the Large Naval Gold Medal and a pension of £3,000 per year (approximately equivalent to about £300,000 per year at 1995 values). He was given the freedom of many cities and boroughs including London, Dundee and Yarmouth. His second-in-command, Vice-Admiral Richard Onslow received a baronetcy and a Large Naval Gold Medal. Captains Trollope and Fairfax were knighted. On 9th May, Lord Duncan received £10,000 as an advance of his share of the prize money (equivalent to about £1,000,000 at 1995 values). A journalist estimated his share would finally amount to about £60,000 but this was never confirmed. Because of the delay and litigation normally associated with such matters, it is unlikely Lord Duncan received all of the prize money in his lifetime. In any event, his mission had not yet been accomplished and he had matters, other than financial ones, on his mind.

Chapter 14 • MISSION ACCOMPLISHED

ILL-HEALTH PREVENTED LORD DUNCAN FROM RETURNING to duty with the North Sea Fleet until the beginning of August 1798 when he hoisted his flag in the *Kent*. This was proving a difficult year for the British Government, faced with armed rebellion in Ireland, with the continuing threat of invasion from across the English Channel and, on the home front, with the need to suppress the rising demand for the formation of trade unions.

A rebellion started in May in Ireland. British troops were widely dispersed throughout the country and they were ill-prepared to deal with such an event. The situation was not improved when Lieutenant-General Sir Ralph Abercrombie, the Commander-in-Chief, tendered his resignation because of his strong objection to the methods proposed by the Irish Government for suppressing the rebellion. It was two months before tranquility was restored to the country.

In March 1798, secret agents notified the British Government that 275,000 French troops were on a twenty-four hour stand-by to proceed to "invasion ports" on the French coast. In addition, it was also believed the French had the capability to land up to 40,000 troops with supporting artillery in Ireland. Whilst Lord Duncan's victory at Camperdown had rescued Britain from the threat of invasion along her East coast from forces based in Holland, it was the job of the Channel Fleet to safeguard the South coast and Ireland from attack.

By the 20th August 1798, Lord Duncan was again standing off the Texel in which fourteen Dutch sails of the line, fourteen frigates, one brig and eighteen transports were lying at anchor. At the time of his appointment to command in the North Sea in 1795, he had been given the task of destroying the enemy fleet. Although he had captured a large number of Dutch ships during the battle in 1797, his mission had still only been partially accomplished.

On the 27th August news came from the Admiralty of three French frigates, all flying the British flag, which had sailed from the Isle of Aix on the 6th August, eluded ships of the Channel Fleet and landed troops in Killala Bay in Ireland on the 22nd August. The French force, under

General of Brigade Humbert, carried muskets and ammunition sufficient to arm four thousand of the local population and Irish recruits had been quick to come forward. On the 27th August, Humbert's troops encountered a British force under the command of Lieutenant General Gerard Lake at Castlebar, twenty miles South of Killala Bay. Lake's force was composed largely of Irish militiamen who, faced with a bayonet charge by battle-hardened French troops, fled in uncontrollable panic to Tuam, thirty miles away. It was not until the 12th September that Humbert's ninety-six officers and eight hundred and forty-four men were eventually forced to surrender having advanced to within sixty miles of Dublin.

Lord Duncan was asked by the Admiralty to prevent supplies and reinforcements for these French forces in Ireland being sent by sea from Holland. The operation in Ireland brought home to Lord Duncan and to the crews of his ships blockading the Texel that the threat of invasion was real. It had only been prevented in the past by their vigilance and by their ships constantly being on duty in the harsh conditions of the North Sea. Lord Duncan and his squadron returned to Yarmouth in the middle of September and the vigil off the Texel was taken over for a number of weeks by Vice-Admiral Sir Richard Onslow's division. In November Sir Richard became ill and resigned, the harsh conditions of life at sea having taken their toll. Lord Duncan returned to Scotland on sick leave, his newly appointed second-in-command, Vice-Admiral Archibald Dickson in the *Monarch*, continuing the surveillance of the Dutch base.

In February of 1799, Lord Duncan was again at sea blockading the Texel. By June, the Admiralty was discussing with him the plan for a landing in Holland to involve both British and Russian army units. There were to be twelve thousand British troops under the command of Lieutenant-General Sir Ralph Abercrombie, with Vice-Admiral Andrew Mitchell responsible for the transport and landing of the troops. Lord Duncan was requested to use his ships to create a diversion. Whilst off the Texel on the 20th August, he encountered the ships of the Expeditionary Force. General Abercrombie and Admiral Mitchell repaired on board the *Kent* when Mitchell explained to him how the troops had embarked at Margate on the 13th August but had been delayed in arriving off the Texel due to adverse wind conditions. General Abercrombie spoke of his intention to land troops on Texel Island and on the Helder Point, operations designed to threaten the Dutch Fleet and the city of Amsterdam.

Knowing how the Dutch Fleet was not keen to engage in battle, Lord Duncan suggested sending in emissaries under a flag of truce asking the Dutch to surrender and offering to treat them as allies should they do so. This was done and their reply was awaited. Over the 21st, 22nd and 23rd August, the wind was in the South West and all ships had to stand off the coast. When received, the Dutch reply was non-committal.

The weather improved on Monday the 26th August and, on the morning of the 27th, after a preparatory bombardment of the beaches, troops landed on Texel Island and Helder Point. There was some heavy fighting until 4 o'clock in the afternoon when the Dutch evacuated Helder and the British took possession. Captured at the same time were thirteen merchantmen, numerous transports and one sixty-four gun, one fifty-four gun, one forty-four gun, one thirty-two gun and three twenty-four gun men-of-war.

On the 30th August, Vice-Admiral Mitchell entered the Texel, at the same time despatching a message to the Dutch Commander, Admiral Storij, demanding the surrender of his fleet. He responded in writing, stating, "The traitors whom I command refused to fight; and nothing remains to me and my brave Officers but vain rage and the dreadful reflection of our present situation : I therefore deliver over to you the Fleet which I commanded." This included one seventy-four gun, five sixty-eight gun, two fifty-four gun, two forty-four gun, one thirty-two gun and one sixteen gun men-of-war.

The Dutch Fleet had surrendered without a shot being fired. Admiral Lord Duncan's mission, defined at the time of his appointment in 1795, had now finally been accomplished. Unfortunately, his lordship had fallen ill on the 30th August and had sailed for home as soon as he saw Vice-Admiral Mitchell's fleet enter the Texel. The First Lord of the Admiralty, Earl Spencer, despatched a letter to Lord Duncan on the 3rd September in which he wrote, "I congratulate you most sincerely on the successful termination of our attack upon the Texel".

The years of service he had spent under appalling conditions on board ship, the inadequacy of the naval diet and the constantly damp atmosphere he had endured, had taken their toll even of his strong constitution. As his health was giving increasing cause for concern, he hauled down his flag in March 1800.

As one Duncan left the naval service another entered. On the 1st April 1800, Lord Duncan's youngest son, fourteen year old Henry (later Captain the Honourable Sir Henry Duncan, K.C.H., C.B., R.N.) joined the *Maidstone* as a midshipman and, by 1803, he was first lieutenant of the *Narcissus* frigate.

The twilight years of Lord Duncan's life were mainly spent at Lundie. The figure head from Admiral de Winter's flagship, the Red Lion of Holland rampant, was brought to Lundie House and the *Vrijheid*'s bell was installed at Lundie Kirk, for many decades summoning worshippers to religious service. Following the death of a relative, the Gleneagles estate passed to Lord Duncan in 1799, it having been in the ownership of his mother's family for six centuries. With estates at Gleneagles and at Lundie and being active in the local kirk, there was much to keep him occupied. His family were growing up and, at the time of his retirement in 1800, the children ranged in age from ten to twenty-two years. Sadly, his eldest son, Alexander, died in Malta in 1803 at the age of twenty-four.

For Admiral Lord Duncan, the call of the sea was still strong even at seventy-three years of age and, in the late summer of 1804, only four years after his retirement, he travelled South to London to offer his services to the Admiralty. On the 4th August 1804, he stopped overnight near Coldstream on his return journey and retired to bed in good spirits after dinner. He was taken ill shortly afterwards and died peacefully before the local doctor could arrive. He lies buried in the tranquility of the little churchyard at Lundie.

On the afternoon of the twenty-fourth November 1804, daylight was fading and a strong north-easterly was blowing in Tor Bay. Vice-Admiral Cornwallis had ordered the fleet to put to sea and set course for Brest. "Anchors secured, sir!" came the call from the *Venerable*'s forecastle.

As the old sail of the line got under way, Captain Hunter realised she was veering towards a vessel on her larboard bow. His crew struggled frantically to control her and to avoid a collision. They knew the rocks of Berry Head lay nearby. There was little room for manoeuvre.

HMS *Venerable* was old and worn but moments of greatness had been hers. An ageing white-haired admiral had controlled her destiny at the time of her greatest victory. He had brought her through a bloody battle with men who had been mutinous only a few weeks before. He had been a kind, gentle, self-effacing, tactful man with nothing bad to say about anyone. He had an intense regard for the officers and men serving under him. He had appreciated the conditions under which they lived and fought. He had given no thought to danger and could withstand hardship with fortitude. He had lived frugally, had a distaste for violence and was a first class seaman.

In his day, he was the most handsome officer in the Royal Navy, six foot four inches tall, proportionately built, dignified with high forehead and fair hair. Together, he and the old ship of the line had saved Great Britain from invasion.

Admiral Lord Duncan and the *Venerable* had been linked inexorably and the old ship was now fighting for survival. On the morning of the 25th November 1804, there was nothing to be seen of her except her bows sticking up out of the water. Four days later she had totally disintegrated. The master and his beloved flagship had now both gone but neither would be forgotten.

His Royal Highness the Duke of Clarence believed Admiral Viscount Duncan's services to his country had never been adequately rewarded. On becoming king, as William IV in 1831, he was graciously pleased to elevate the admiral's son, Robert Dundas Duncan, the Second Viscount, to the Earldom of Camperdown. It was Robert who built Camperdown House on the Lundie estate in 1823. The title survived only until the death in 1933 of the admiral's great-grandson, George Alexander Duncan, the Fourth Earl. Around 1918, the Lundie estate passed to the admiral's great-granddaughter, Georgina Wilhelmina Mercer-Henderson, the Countess of Buckingham. Camperdown House was sold to Dundee Corporation in 1946 and the Lundie Estate was sold in 1972.

Jack Crawford, the sailor who nailed Admiral Duncan's flag to the mast during the Battle of Camperdown, was awarded a medal by the Town of Sunderland. On the reverse of the medal is a scene of the action with, above, the legend "DUNCAN AND GLORY" and below "BRITISH VALOUR".

In 1848, approval was given for the award to those present at specific actions between 1793 and 1840, of a Naval General Service Medal with named bars. Awards were made only to those who were living in 1848. Eighteen members of the crew of the *Venerable* were still alive at that time, fifty-one years after the battle, and they received the medal with the CAMPERDOWN bar. They were:-

James Aitken	Ordinary	John Robert Gould	Boatswain
William Balchin	Boy	Thomas Harford	Pte. R.M.
William Clark	Boy	John Hatton	Ordinary
Thomas Ellis	Boy	Charles Hutchins	Landsman
Gordon Falcon	Master's Mate	John Neale	Mids'man
Benjamin Robinson	A.B.	John Fiffe	Landsman
John Rose	A.B.	William Fig	A.B.
James Smith	Ordinary	Edward Frost	A.B.
John Smith	Landsman	John Webber	Coxswain

Of the fifteen thousand men forming the crews of the twenty-five ships which took part in the Battle of Camperdown, two hundred and ninety-eight were still alive in 1848 and they received the Naval General Service Medal 1793-1840 with the CAMPERDOWN bar.

Undoubtedly, Admiral Lord Duncan would have approved of his "lads" being honoured in this way.

REFERENCES

Baynham, H. *Before the Mast*, Hutchinson, London, 1971

Baynham, H. *From the Lower Deck. The Old Navy 1780-1841*, Hutchinson, London, 1969

Camperdown, Earl of, Admiral Duncan, Longmans, Green & Co., London, 1898

Clowes, W.L. *The Royal Navy, A History from Earliest Times to the Present*, Sampson, Low Marston & Co, 1898

Cooper, J. Fennimore *The Pathfinder*, Everyman's Library, London, Reprint 1968

Corbett, Sir J.S. England in *The Seven Years' War (A Study of Combined Strategy)* Vols I, II, Longmans, Green & Co., London 1918

Corbett, J.S. (Editor) *The Spencer Papers*, Naval Research 1894, Vols 1, 2.

Duncan Papers at the National Maritime Museum

Earle, P. Corsairs of Malta and Barbary, Sidgwick & Jackson, London, 1970

Elliott, A. *Hood in Scotland*. James P Matthew, Dundee, 1885

Erskine, D. *Augustus Hervey's Journals*, William Kimber, London, 1953

Gibson, J.S. *Ships of the '45*, Hutchinson & Co, London, 1967

Hampshire, A.C. *Just an Old Navy Custom*, William Kimber, London, 1979

Hart, F.R. *The The Siege of Havana*, Houghton, Mifflin Co., George Allen & Unwin, Ltd, London 1931

Hutchinson, W. *A Treatise of Practical Seamanship (1777)*, Scolar Press, London, 1979

Julien, C.A. (translated by John Petrie) *History of North Africa* (Editor C.C. Stewart), Routledge and Kegan Paul, London 1931 (French); 1970

Kay, B. (Editor) *The Dundee Book*, Mainstream Publishing, 1990

Kemp, P. *History of the Royal Navy*, Arthur Baker, Ltd., London, 1969

Kennedy, P.M. *The Rise and Fall of British Naval Mastery*, Allen Lane and Penguin Books, 1976

Keppel, Hon. Rev. T. *The Life of Augustus Keppel*, Henry Colbury, London,1842

Lloyd, C. *Captain Marryat and the Navy*, Longmans, Green and Co., London, 1939

Lloyd, C. *St. Vincent and Camperdown*, B.T. Batsford, London, 1940

Lords Commissioners of the Admiralty, *Manual of Seamanship*, Vol. 1, 1908

Lords Commissioners of the Admiralty, *A Seaman's Pocket-Book*, June 1943

MacArthur, Lt-Gen Sir W. *The Appin Murder and The Trial of James Stewart*, J.M.P. Publishing Services, London, 1960

Manwaring, G.E. and B. Dobree *The Floating Republic*, Frank Cass & Co Ltd, London, 1966

Marriner, J. *Sailing to Timbuctu*, William Kimber, London, 1973

McGuffie, T.H. *The Siege of Gibraltar*, 1779-1783, B.T. Batsford, London, 1965

Morgan, K.O. (Editor) *The Oxford Illustrated History of Britain*, Oxford University Press, 1984

Nelson, N. *Tunisia*, B.T. Batsford, London, 1974

Padfield, P *Tide of Empires*, Routledge and Kegan Paul, London, 1982

Parkinson C. *Northcote The Fireship*, John Murray, 1975

Pearse, Colonel H. *Memoir of the Life and Military Service of Viscount Lake, Baron Lake of Delhi and Laswaree 1744-1808*, William Blackwood and Sons, Edinburgh and London, 1908

Richmond, Rear-Admiral H.W. *The Navy in the War of 1739-48*, Cambridge University Press, 1920

Sinclair Sir J. (Editor) *The Statistical Account of Scotland, 1791-1799*, Vol. X Fife, EP Publishing Ltd, 1978

Smith, A. 'Dundee and the '45' (from *The '45, To Gather An Image* edited by Lesley Scott-Moncrieff, Mercat Press, 1988)

Smout, T.C. *A History of the Scottish People 1560-1830*, William Collins & Sons, 1969

Stewart, Colonel David, *Sketches of the Character, Manners and Present State of the Highlanders of Scotland*, 1822, reprinted by John Donald Publishers, Edinburgh, 1977

Styles, S. *Sea Road to Camperdown*, Faber and Faber, London, 1968

Syrett, D. *The Siege and Capture of Havana*, 1762, Navy Records Society, 1970

Tullibardine, Marchioness of, *A Military History of Perthshire 1899-1902* (Paper by Eleanor C. Sellar)

Walker, Lt-Comdr C.F. *Young Gentlemen*, Longmans, Green and Co., London, 1938

Walter, R. *Lord Anson's Voyage Round the World 1740-1744*, Penguin Books, 1947

Walton, T. *Know Your Ship*, Chas. Griffin & Co, London, 1896

Watts, A.J. *Pictorial History of the Royal Navy*, Ian Allan, London, 1970

Young, Brigadier Peter and Lt-Col J.P. Lawford *History of The British Army*, Arthur Barker Ltd, London, 1970

INDEX